Morning Yet on Creation Day

MORNING YET
ON
CREATION DAY

Essays

CHINUA ACHEBE

ANCHOR PRESS/DOUBLEDAY

GARDEN CITY, NEW YORK

1975

Library of Congress Cataloging in Publication Data

Achebe, Chinua
  Morning yet on creation day

  1.   African literature (English)—History and criticism—Addresses, es-
says, lectures. 2.   African literature—History and criticism—Addresses, es-
says, lectures.
I.   Title.
PB9340.5.A3   820'.9'96
ISBN 0-385-01703-0
Library of Congress Catalog Card Number 74-33603

Baa, baa, black sheep,
Have you any wool?
Yes, sir, yes, sir, three bags full.

To the memory of Harvey Swados

and for

Priscilla Tyler
Ulli Beier
Sam Nwoye

Essays

PART ONE

PART TWO

Preface

A writer need never offer excuses for writing. But under certain conditions he may feel that some explanation is in order for the publication of what he has written, or the reissuing of it after the impulse and circumstance of its original composition have passed. Should any doubt arise in his mind on this score, his resolution of it (if he is at all like me) will turn largely on public interest. And I mean *interest* in both its senses.

Two or three of the items in this collection will bring back unhappy memories of our country's recent past, and I have no doubt that there will be some inclined to the view that it were better to forget the agonies of that past and turn the mind to the marvelous achievements of "reconciliation, rehabilitation, and reconstruction." I do not agree. I believe that in our situation the greater danger lies not in remembering but in forgetting, in pretending that slogans are the same as truth; and I believe that Ni-

geria, always prone to self-deception, stands in great need
of reminders.

Experience is necessary for growth and survival, but experience is not simply what happened. A lot may happen
to a piece of stone without making it any wiser. Experience is what we are able and prepared to do with what
happens to us. A Nigerian was asked what he considered
the big lesson of the civil war and he replied with typical
smugness: "Secession does not pay." I believe that if we
are to survive as a nation, we need to grasp the meaning
of our tragedy. One way to do it is to remind ourselves
constantly of the things that happened and how we felt
when they were happening.

The open letter to Mr. Tai Solarin now sounds shrill in
my ears and I did think seriously of leaving it out, especially as I regard Mr. Solarin as a rare and hopeful phenomenon in Nigeria—an intellectual with enough guts to
speak his mind. But his article which prompted my letter
was, in the charged moments of 1966, a horrendous mis-
judgment. In deciding to bring back that whole episode,
I have chosen to be accused of strident anger and nasti-
ness rather than join in the current national pastime of
consigning ten years ago into prehistory.

The more purely literary essays (although I doubt that
anything I have ever written could pass the purity test)
pose a different kind of problem in our rapidly evolving
situation. On rereading one or two of the earlier pieces,
I have felt uneasy in places. For example, the fatalistic
logic of the unassailable position of English in our literature leaves me more cold now than it did when I first

spoke about it in the auditorium of the University of Ghana with that formidable Irishman, Conor Cruise O'Brien, in the chair and the great African revolutionary, Kwame Nkrumah, in Flagstaff House. And yet I am unable to see a significantly different or a more emotionally comfortable resolution of that problem.

University of Massachusetts

Amherst

June 1974

Morning Yet on Creation Day

PART 1

COLONIALIST CRITICISM

The word *colonialist* may be deemed inappropriate for two reasons. First, it has come to be associated in many minds with that brand of cheap, demagogic, and outmoded rhetoric which the distinguished Ghanaian public servant, Robert Gardiner, no doubt has in mind when he speaks of our tendency to "intone the colonial litany," implying that the time has come when we must assume responsibility for our problems and our situation in the world and resist the temptation to blame other people. Secondly, it may be said that whatever colonialism may have done in the past, the very fact of a Commonwealth Conference today[1] is sufficient repudiation of it, is indeed a symbol of a new relationship of equality between people who were once masters and servants.

Yet in spite of the strength of these arguments one feels the necessity to deal with some basic issues raised by a certain specious criticism which flourishes in African liter-

[1] This essay is based on a paper read to the Association for Commonwealth Literature and Language Studies at Makerere University, Uganda, in January 1974.

ature today and which derives from the same basic attitude and assumption as colonialism itself and so merits
the name *colonialist*. This attitude and assumption were
crystallized in Albert Schweitzer's immortal dictum in the
heyday of colonialism: *The African is indeed my brother,
but my junior brother.* The latter-day colonialist critic
equally given to big-brother arrogance sees the African
writer as a somewhat unfinished European who with patient guidance will grow up one day and write like every
other European, but meanwhile must be humble, must
learn all he can and, while at it, give due credit to his
teachers in the form of either direct praise or, even better, since praise sometimes goes bad and becomes em-
barrassing, manifest self-contempt. Because of the tricky
nature of this subject, I have chosen to speak not in general terms but, wherever possible, specifically about my
own actual experience. In any case, as anyone who has
heard anything at all about me may know already, I do
have problems with universality and other concepts of
that scope, being very much a down-to-earth person. But
I will hope by reference to a few other writers and critics
to show that my concerns and anxieties are perhaps not
entirely personal.

When my first novel was published in 1958, a very unusual review of it was written by a British woman, Honor
Tracy, who is perhaps not so much a critic as a literary
journalist. But what she said was so intriguing that I have
never forgotten it. If I remember rightly she headlined
it "Three cheers for mere Anarchy!" The burden of the
review itself was as follows: These bright Negro barristers[2] who talk so glibly about African culture, how would

---

[2] How barristers came into it remains a mystery to me to this day, but I
have sometimes woven fantasies about an earnest white woman and an
unscrupulous black barrister.

they like to return to wearing raffia skirts? How would novelist Achebe like to go back to the mindless times of his grandfather instead of holding the modern job he has in broadcasting in Lagos?

I should perhaps point out that colonialist criticism is not always as crude as this, but the exaggerated grossness of a particular example may prove useful in studying the anatomy of the species. There are three principal parts here: Africa's inglorious past (raffia skirts) to which Europe brings the blessing of civilization (Achebe's modern job in Lagos) and for which Africa returns ingratitude (skeptical novels like *Things Fall Apart*).

Before I go on to more advanced varieties I must give one more example of the same kind as Honor Tracy's which on account of its recentness (1970) actually surprised me.

The British administration not only safe-guarded women from the worst tyrannies of their masters, it also enabled them to make their long journeys to farm or market without armed guard, secure from the menace to hostile neighbors. . . . The Nigerian novelists, who have written the charming and bucolic accounts of domestic harmony in African rural communities, are the sons whom the labors of these women educated; the peaceful village of their childhood to which they nostalgically look back was one which had been purged of bloodshed and alcoholism by an ague-ridden district officer and a Scottish mission lassie whose years were cut short by every kind of intestinal parasite.

It is even true to say that one of the most nostalgically convincing of the rural African novelists used as his

sourcebook not the memories of his grandfathers but
the records of the despised British anthropologists.
. . . The modern African mythmaker hands down
a vision of colonial rule in which the native powers
are chivalrously viewed through the eyes of the hard-
won liberal tradition of the late Victorian scholar,
while the expatriates are shown as schoolboys' black-
board caricatures.

Iris Andreski: *Old Wives' Tales*

I have quoted this at such length because first of all I am
intrigued by Iris Andreski's literary style which recalls
so faithfully the sedate prose of the district-officer-
government-anthropologist of sixty or seventy years ago
—a tribute to her remarkable powers of identification as
well as to the durability of colonialist rhetoric. *Tyrannies of their masters. Menace of hostile neighbors.
Purged of bloodshed and alcoholism.* But in addition to
this, Iris Andreski advances the position taken by Honor
Tracy in one significant and crucial direction—its claim
to a deeper knowledge and a more reliable appraisal of
Africa than the educated African writer has shown himself capable of.

To the colonialist mind it was always of the utmost importance to be able to say: *I know my natives,* a claim
which implied two things at once: (a) that the native
was really quite simple and (b) that understanding him
and controlling him went hand in hand—understanding
being a precondition for control and control constituting
adequate proof of understanding. Thus in the heyday of
colonialism any serious incident of native unrest, carrying as it did disquieting intimations of slipping control,

was an occasion not only for pacification by the soldiers but also (afterwards) for a royal commission of inquiry —a grand name for yet another perfunctory study of native psychology and institutions. Meanwhile a new situation was slowly developing as a handful of natives began to acquire European education and then to challenge Europe's presence and position in their native land with the intellectual weapons of Europe itself. To deal with this phenomenal presumption, the colonialist devised two contradictory arguments. He created the "man of two worlds" theory to prove that no matter how much the native was exposed to European influences he could never truly absorb them; like Prester John he would always discard the mask of civilization when the crucial hour came and reveal his true face. Now, did this mean that the educated native was no different at all from his brothers in the bush? Oh, no! He *was* different; he was worse. His abortive effort at education and culture, though leaving him totally unredeemed and unregenerated, had nonetheless done something to him—it had deprived him of his links with his own people whom he no longer even understood and who certainly wanted none of his dissatisfaction or pretensions. *I know my natives; they are delighted with the way things are. It's only these half-educated ruffians, who don't even know their own people.* . . . How often one heard that and the many variations of it in colonial times! And how almost amusing to find its legacy in the colonialist criticism of our literature today! Iris Andreski's book is more than old wives' tales, at least in intention. It is clearly inspired by the desire to undercut the educated African witness (the modern mythmaker, she calls him) by appealing directly to the unspoilt woman of the bush who has retained a healthy gratitude for Europe's intervention in Africa. This desire accounts for all that reliance one finds in modern European travelers' tales on the evidence of *simple natives*—houseboys, cooks, drivers, schoolchildren—supposedly more trustworthy than the smart alecks. An American critic, Charles Larson, makes good use of this kind of evidence not only to validate his literary opinion of Ghana's Ayi Kwei Armah, but, even more important, to demonstrate its superiority over the opinion of Ghanaian intellectuals.

> When I asked a number of students at the University of Ghana about their preferences for contemporary African novelists, Ayi Kwei Armah was the writer mentioned most frequently, in spite of the fact that many of Ghana's older writers and intellectuals regard him as a kind of negativist. . . . I have for some time regarded Ayi Kwei Armah as Anglophone Africa's most accomplished prose stylist.[3]

In 1962 I published an essay, *Where Angels Fear to Tread*, in which I suggested that the European critic of African literature must cultivate the habit of humility appropriate to his limited experience of the African world and be purged of the superiority and arrogance which history so insidiously makes him heir to. That article, though couched in very moderate terms, won for me quite a few bitter enemies. One of them took my comments so badly—almost as a personal affront—that he launched numerous unprovoked attacks against me. Well, he has recently come to grief by his own hand. He published a long abstruse treatise based on an analysis

[3] *Books Abroad*, Winter 1974.

of a number of Igbo proverbs most of which, it turned out, he had so completely misunderstood as to translate "fruit" in one of them as "penis." Whereupon, a merciless native, less charitable than I, proceeded to make mincemeat of him. If only he had listened to me ten years ago!

In his book *Homecoming*, Ngugi wa Thiongo pays some attention to this kind of "African expert" and his pretensions to superior knowledge:

> Some of these people, once described by Jomo Kenyatta as professional friends and interpreters of the African, have the arrogance of assuming that they have more and closer ties to Africa than have Africans in the West Indies and in America. It is such people who acquire a most proprietorial air when talking of the part of Africa they have happened to visit; they carve a personal sphere of influence and champion the most reactionary and the most separatist cause of whichever group among whom they happen to live. They are again the most vehement in pointing out the unique intelligence, amiability and quick wit of their adopted areas and groups. We must never succumb to the poisonous and divisive flattery of our enemies.
>
> (pages xviii–xix)

Ngugi is clearly talking in broader terms than just literature, but his description fits the colonialist critic quite well. After the publication of *A Man of the People* in 1966, I was invited to dinner by a British diplomat in Lagos at which his wife, hitherto a fan of mine, admonished me for what she called "this great disservice to Nigeria." She loved Nigeria so much that my criticisms of the country which ignored all the brave efforts it was making left her totally aghast. I told her something not very nice, and our friendship was brought to an end. She was of course only a housewife and not a critic, but colonialist critics and colonialist housewives ultimately speak a common language. Last year a critic, not a housewife, in Britain, writing about my poems in which he saw no merit whatever (which was entirely within his rights), went on to deplore the fact that I had evaded the responsibility to "challenge the soul of Nigeria." This was not within his rights. In fact it is the height of impertinence. For who is this man to tell me when and how the soul of Nigeria is to be challenged? Who is this sympathizer whose weeping is so loud that he drowns the owners of the corpse?

Most African writers write out of an African experience and of commitment to an African destiny. For them that destiny does not include a future European identity for which the present is but an apprenticeship. And let no one be fooled by the fact that we may write in English, for we intend to do unheard of things with it. Already some people are getting worried. This past summer I met one of Australia's leading poets, A. D. Hope, in Canberra, and he said wistfully that the only happy writers today were those writing in small languages like Danish. Why? Because they and their readers understood one another and knew precisely what a word meant when it was used. I had to admit that I hadn't thought of it that way. I had always assumed that the Commonwealth of Nations was a great bonus for a writer, that the English-speaking Union was a desirable fraternity. But talking with A. D. Hope that evening, I felt somewhat like an illegitimate child, face to face with the true son of the house, lamenting the excesses of an adventurous and profligate father who had kept a mistress in every port. I felt momentarily nasty and thought of telling A. D. Hope: You ain't seen nothin' yet! But I know he would not have understood. And in any case, there was an important sense in which he was right—that every literature must seek the things that belong unto its peace, must, in other words, speak of a particular place, evolve out of the necessities of its history, past and current, and the aspirations and destiny of its people.

Australia proved quite enlightening.[4] On another occasion, a student at the National University who had taken a course in African literature asked me if the time had not come for African writers to write about "people in general" instead of just Africans. I asked her if by *people in general* she meant *like Australians,* and gave her the bad news that as far as I was concerned such a time would never come. She was only a brash sophomore. But like all the other women I have referred to, she expressed herself with passionate and disarming effrontery. I don't know how women's lib will take this, but I do believe that by and large women are more honest than men in expressing their feelings. This woman was only making the same point which many "serious" critics have been making more tactfully and therefore more insidiously. They dress it up in fine robes which they call universality.

In his book, *The Emergence of African Fiction,* Charles

[4] I hope I do not sound too ungracious. Certainly I met very many fine and sensitive people in Australia; and the words which the distinguished historian, Professor Manning Clark, wrote to me after my visit are among the finest tributes I have ever received: "I hope you come back and speak again here, because we need to lose the blinkers of our past. So come and help the young to grow up without the prejudices of their forefathers. . . ."

Larson tells us a few revealing things about universality. In a chapter devoted to Lenrie Peters' novel, which he finds particularly impressive, he speaks of "its universality, its very limited concern with Africa itself." Then he goes on to spell it all out:

> That it is set in Africa appears to be accidental, for, except for a few comments at the beginning, Peters' story might just as easily take place in the southern part of the United States or, in the southern regions of France or Italy. If a few names of characters and places were changed, one would indeed feel that this was an American novel. In short, Peters' story is universal.[5]

But Larson is obviously not as foolish as this passage would make him out to be, for he ends it on a note of self-doubt which I find totally disarming. He says:

> Or am I deluding myself in considering the work universal. Maybe what I really mean is that *The Second Round* is to a great degree Western and therefore scarcely African at all.

I find it hard after that to show more harshness than merely agreeing about his delusion. But few people I know are prepared to be so charitable. In a recent review of the book in *Okike*, a Nigerian critic, Omolara Leslie, mocks "the shining faith that we are all Americans under the skin."

Does it ever occur to the Larsons of African literature

[5] Charles Larson, *The Emergence of African Fiction*. Bloomington: Indiana University Press, 1971, p. 230.

to try out their game of changing names of characters and places in an American novel, say, a Philip Roth or an Updike, and slotting in African names just to see how it works? But of course it would not occur to them. It would never occur to them to doubt the universality of their own literature. In the nature of things, the work of a Western writer is automatically informed by universality. It is only others who must strain to achieve it. So-and-So's work is universal; he has truly arrived! As though universality were some distant bend in the road which you may take if you travel out far enough in the direction of Europe or America, if you put adequate distance between you and your home. I should like to see the word *universal* banned altogether from discussions of African literature until such a time as people cease to use it as a synonym for the narrow, self-serving parochialism of Europe, until their horizon extends to include all the world.

If colonialist criticism were merely irritating, one might doubt the justification of devoting a whole essay to it. But strange though it may sound, some of its ideas and precepts do exert an influence on our writers, for it is a fact of our contemporary world that Europe's powers of persuasion can be far in excess of the merit and value of her case. Take for instance the black writer who seizes on the theme that "Africa's past is a sadly inglorious one" as though it were something new that had not already been "proved" adequately for him. Colonialist critics will, of course, fall all over him in ecstatic and salivating admiration—which is neither unexpected nor particularly interesting. What is fascinating, however, is the tortuous logic and sophistry they will sometimes weave around a perfectly straightforward and natural enthusiasm.

A review of Yambo Ouologuem's *Bound to Violence* by a Philip M. Allen in the *Pan-African Journal* (Fall 1971) was an excellent example of sophisticated, even brilliant, colonialist criticism. The opening sentence alone would reward long and careful examination; but I shall content myself here with merely quoting it:

> The achievement of Ouologuem's much discussed impressive, yet overpraised novel has less to do with whose ideological team he's playing on than with the *forcing of moral universality on African civilization.* (my italics)

A little later Mr. Allen expounds on this new moral universality:

> This morality is not only "un-African"—denying the standards set by omnipresent ancestors, the solidarity of communities, the legitimacy of social contract: it is a Hobbesian universe that extends beyond the wilderness, beyond the white man's myths of Africa, into all civilization, theirs and ours.

If you should still be wondering at this point how Ouologuem was able to accomplish that herculean feat of forcing moral universality on Africa, or with what gargantuan tools, Mr. Allen quickly relieves your suspense. Ouologuem is "an African intellectual who has mastered both a style and a prevailing philosophy of French letters," able to enter "the remoter alcoves of French philosophical discourse."

Mr. Allen is quite abrupt in dismissing all the "various polemical factions" and ideologists who have been claiming Ouologuem for their side. Of course they all miss the point.

> for Ouologuem isn't writing their novel. He gives us an Africa cured of the pathetic obsession with racial and cultural confrontation and freed from invidious tradition-mongering. . . . His book knows no easy antithesis between white and black, Western and indigenous, modern and traditional. Its conflicts are those of the universe, not accidents of history.

And in final demonstration of Ouologuem's liberation from the constraint of local models, Mr. Allen tells us:

> Ouologuem does not accept Fanon's idea of liberation, and he calls African unity a theory for dreamers. His Nakem is no more the Mali of Modibo Keita or the continent of Nkrumah than is the golden peace of Emperor Sundiata or the moral parish of Muntu.

Mr. Allen's rhetoric does not entirely conceal whose ideological team *he* is playing on, his attitude to Africa, in other words. Note, for example, the significant antithesis between the infinite space of "a Hobbesian universe" and "the moral parish of Muntu" with its claustrophobic implications. Who but Western Man could contrive such arrogance?

Running through Mr. Allen's review is the overriding thesis that Ouologuem has somehow restored dignity to his people and their history by investing them with responsibility for violence and evil. Mr. Allen returns to this thesis again and again, merely changing the form of words. And we are to understand, by fairly clear implication, that this was something brave and new for Africa, this manly assumption of responsibility.

Of course a good deal of colonialist rhetoric always turned on that very question—the moral inferiority of colonized peoples of which subjugation was a prime consequence and penalty was most clearly demonstrated in their unwillingness to assume roles of responsibility. As long ago (or as recently, depending on one's historical perspective) as 1910, the popular English novelist John Buchan wrote a colonialist classic, *Prester John*, in which we find the words:

> That is the difference between white and black, the gift of responsibility.

And the idea did not originate with Buchan, either. It was a foundation tenet of colonialism and a recurrent element of its ideology and rhetoric. Now, to tell a man that he is incapable of assuming responsibility for himself and his actions is of course the utmost insult, to avoid which, some Africans will go to any length, will throw anything into the deal; they will agree, for instance, to ignore the presence and role of racism in African history or pretend that somehow it was all the black man's own fault. Which is complete and utter nonsense. For whatever faults the black man may have or whatever crimes he committed (and they were, and are, legion), he did not bring racism into the world. And no matter how emancipated a man may wish to appear, or how anxious to please by his largeness of heart, he cannot make history simply go away. Not even a brilliant writer could hope to do that. And as for those who applaud him for trying, who acclaim his bold originality in "restoring historical initiative to his people" when in reality all he does is pander to their racist and colonialist attitudes, they are no more than unscrupulous interrogators taking advantage of an ingratiating defendant's weakness and trust to egg him on to irretrievable self-incrimination.

That a "critic" playing on the ideological team of colonialism should feel sick and tired of Africa's "pathetic obsession with racial-cultural confrontation" should surprise no one. Neither should his enthusiasm for those African works that show "no easy antithesis between white and black." But an African who falls for such nonsense, not only in spite of Africa's so very recent history but, even more, in the face of continuing atrocities committed against millions of Africans in their own land by racist minority regimes, deserves a lot of pity. Certainly anyone, white or black, who chooses to see violence as the abiding principle of African civilization is free to do so. But let him not pass himself off as a restorer of dignity to Africa, or attempt to make out that he is writing about Man and about the state of civilization in general.[6] The futility of such service to Africa, leaving aside any question of duplicity in the motive, should be sufficiently underscored by one interesting admission in Mr. Allen's review:

Thus, there is no reason for Western reviewers of this book to exult in a black writer's admission of the savagery, sensuality and amorality of his race: he isn't talking about his race as Senghor or Cleaver do: he's talking about us all.

[6] You could as well claim that fifty years ago Frank Melland's *In Witchbound Africa* was an account of the universality of witchcraft and a vindication of Africa.

Well, how obtuse of these "Western reviewers" to miss that point and draw such wrong conclusions! But the trouble is that not everyone can be as bright as Mr. Allen. Perhaps for most ordinary people what Africa needs is a far less complicated act of restoration. The Canadian novelist and critic, Margaret Laurence, saw this happening already in the way many African writers are interpreting their world, making it

> neither idyllic, as the views of some nationalists would have had it, nor barbaric, as the missionaries and European administrators wished and needed to believe.[7]

And in the epilogue to the same book she makes the point even more strongly:

> No writer of any quality has viewed the old Africa in an idealized way, but they have tried to regain what is rightly theirs—a past composed of real and vulnerable people, their ancestors, not the figments of missionary and colonialist imaginations.

Ultimately the question of ideological sides which Mr. Allen threw in, only to dismiss again with contempt, may not be as far-fetched as he thinks, for colonialism itself was built also on an ideology (although its adherents may no longer realize it) which, despite many setbacks, survives into our own day, indeed is ready again at the end of a quiescent phase of self-doubt for a new resur-

---

[7] Margaret Laurence, *Long Drums and Cannons*. New York: Macmillan, 1968, p. 9.

gence of proselytization, even, as in the past, among its prime victims!

Fortunately, it can no longer hope for the role of un-challenged arbiter in other people's affairs that it once took so much for granted. There are clear signs that crit-ics and readers from those areas of the world, where continuing incidents and recent memories of racism, colo-nialism, and other forms of victimization exist, will more and more demand to know from their writers just on whose ideological side they are playing. And we writers had better be prepared to reckon with this questioning. For no amount of prestige or laurels of metropolitan rep-utation would seem large enough to silence or overawe it. Consider, for instance, a recent judgment on V. S. Naipaul by a fellow Caribbean, Ivan Van Sertima:

> His brilliancy of wit I do not deny but, in my opinion, he has been overrated by English critics whose sensi-bilities he insidiously flatters by his stock in trade: self-contempt.[8]

A Nigerian, Ime Ikkideh, was even less ceremonious in his dismissal of Naipaul whom he thought did not de-serve the attention paid to him by Ngugi wa Thiongo in his *Homecoming*.[9] One need not accept these judgments in order to see them as signs of things to come.

Meanwhile the seduction of our writers by the blan-dishments of colonialist criticism is matched by its misdi-rection of our critics. Thus an intelligent man like Dr. Sunday Anozie, the Nigerian scholar and critic, is able

---

[8] Ivan Van Sertima, *Caribbean Writers*. Boston: Beacon Press, 1968, Foreword.

[9] Ngugi wa Thiongo, *Homecoming*. Heinemann, 1972, p. xiv.

to dismiss the high moral and social earnestness sometimes expressed by one of our greatest poets, Christopher
Okigbo, as only a mark of underdevelopment. In his
book, *Christopher Okigbo*, the most extensive biograph-
ical and critical study of the poet to date, Dr. Anozie
tells us of Okigbo's "passion for truth" which apparently
makes him sometimes too outspoken, makes him the talk-
ative weaverbird "incapable of whispered secrets." And
he proceeds to offer the following explanation:

> No doubt the thrill of actualized prophecy can some-
> times lead poets particularly in the young countries
> to confuse their role with that of seers, and novelists
> to see themselves as teachers. Whatever the social,
> psychological, political and economic basis for it in
> present-day Africa, this interchangeability of role be-
> tween the creative writer and the prophet appears
> to be a specific phenomenon of underdevelopment
> and therefore, like it also, a passing or ephemeral
> phase.[10]

And he cites the authority of C. M. Bowra in support of
his explanation. The fallacy of the argument lies, of
course, in its assumption that when you talk about a people's *level of development* you define their total condition and assign them an indisputable and unambiguous
place on mankind's evolutionary ladder; in other words,
that you are enabled by the authority of that phrase to
account for all their material as well as spiritual circumstance. Show me a people's plumbing, you say, and I can
tell you their art.

[10] Sunday O. Anozie, *Christopher Okigbo*. New York: Evans Brothers,
1972, p. 17.

I should have thought that the very example of the Hebrew poet/prophets which Dr. Anozie takes from Bowra to demonstrate underdevelopment and confusion of roles would have been enough to alert him to the folly of his thesis. Or is he seriously suggesting that the poetry of these men—Isaiah, for example—written, it seems, out of a confusion of roles, in an underdeveloped society, is less good than what is written today by poets who are careful to remain within the proper bounds of poetry within developed societies? Personally I should be quite content to wallow in Isaiah's error and write *For unto us a child is born.*

Incidentally any reader who is at all familiar with some of the arguments that go on around modern African literature will have noticed that in the passage I have just quoted from Dr. Anozie, he is talking not only about Okigbo but also alluding (with some disapproval) to a paper I read at Leeds University ten years ago which I called "The Novelist as Teacher"; Anozie thus kills two weaverbirds dexterously with one stone! In his disapproval of what I had to say he follows, of course, in the footsteps of certain Western literary schoolmasters, from whom I had already earned many sharp reprimands for that paper, who told me in clear terms that an artist had no business being so earnest.

It seems to me that this matter is of serious and fundamental importance and must be looked at carefully. Earnestness and its opposite, levity, may be neither good nor bad in themselves but merely appropriate or inappropriate according to circumstance. I hold, however, and have held from the very moment I began to write, that earnestness *is* appropriate to my situation. Why? I suppose because I have a deep-seated need to alter things within that situation, to find for myself a little more room than has been allowed me in the world. I realize how pompous or even frightening this must sound to delicate sensibilities, but I can't help it.

The missionary who left the comforts of Europe to wander through my primeval forest was extremely earnest. He had to be; he came to change my world. The builders of empire who turned me into a *British protected person* knew the importance of being earnest; they had that quality of mind which Imperial Rome before them understood so well: *gravitas*. Now, it seems to me pretty obvious that if I desire to change the role and identity fashioned for me by those earnest agents of colonialism I will need to borrow some of their resolve. Certainly I could not hope to do it through self-indulgent levity.

But of course I do appreciate also that the world is large and that all men cannot be, indeed must not be, of one mind. I appreciate that there are people in the world who have no need or desire to change anything. Perhaps they have already accomplished the right amount of change to insure their own comfort. Perhaps they see the need for change but feel powerless to attempt it, or perhaps they feel it is someone else's business. For these people, earnestness is a dirty word or is simply tiresome. Even the evangelist, once so earnest and certain, now sits back in contemplation of his church, its foundation well and truly laid, its edifice rising majestically where once was jungle; the colonial governor who once brought his provinces so ruthlessly to heel prefers now to speak of the benefits of peace and orderly government. Certainly they will much rather have easygoing natives under their jurisdiction than earnest ones—unless of course the earnestness be the perverse kind that turns in against itself.

The first nationalists and freedom fighters in the colonies, hardly concerned to oblige their imperial masters, were offensively earnest. They had no choice. They needed to alter the arrangement which kept them and their people out in the rain and the heat of the sun. They fought and won some victories. They changed a few things and seemed to secure certain powers of action over others. But quite quickly the great collusive swindle that was independence showed its true face to us. And we were dismayed; but only momentarily, for even in our defeat we had gained something of inestimable value— a baptism of fire.

And so our world stands in just as much need of change today as it ever did in the past. Our writers responding to something in themselves and acting also within the traditional concept of an artist's role in society—using his art to control his environment—have addressed themselves to some of these matters in their art. And their concern seems to upset certain people whom history has dealt with differently and who persist in denying the validity of experiences and destinies other than theirs. And, worst of all, some of our own critics who ought to guide these people out of their error seem so anxious to oblige them. Whatever the social, psychological, political, and economic basis for this acquiescence one hopes that it is only a passing and an ephemeral phase!

If this earnestness we speak of were manifested by just one or two writers in Africa, there might perhaps be a good case for dismissing it out of hand. But look at the evidence:

Amos Tutuola has often given as a reason for his writing the need to preserve his traditional culture. It is true that a foreign critic, Adrian Roscoe, has chosen to jubilate over what appears to him to be Tutuola's lack of "an awareness of cultural, national, and racial affinities,"[11] but such an opinion may reflect more accurately his own wishful thinking than Tutuola's mind. Certainly a careful reading of The Palm-Wine Drinkard will not bear out the assertion that colonialism is "dead for him." Why would he go out of his way to tell us, for example, that "both white and black deads were living in the Deads' Town"[12] unless he considers the information significant as indeed anyone who lived in the Lagos of the fifties would readily appreciate, for although Nigeria experienced only "benign colonialism," it required a monumental demonstration of all nationalist organizations in the territory, after a particularly blatant incident of racism in a Lagos hotel, to compel the administration into token relaxation of the practice whereby whites and blacks lived in trim reservations or squalid townships separated by a regulation two-mile cordon sanitaire. Someday a serious critic interested in such matters will assemble and interpret Tutuola's many scattered allusions to colonialism for the benefit of more casual readers. For there are such intriguing incidents as the Drinkard's deliverance of the Red People from an ancient terror which required them to sacrifice one victim every year, for which blessing he lives among them for a while, exploiting their cheap labor to develop and extend his plantations, "becoming richer than the rest of the people in that town" until the moment of crisis arrives and he causes

[11] Adrian A. Roscoe, Mother Is Gold. London: Cambridge University Press, 1971, pp. 98–99.
[12] Amos Tutuola, The Palm-Wine Drinkard. Grove Press, 1953, p. 100.

"the whole of them" to be wiped out. Such a critic will
no doubt pay particular attention to the unperturbed
and laconic comment of the deliverer's wife: ". . . all the
lives of the natives were lost and the lives of the non-
natives saved."[13] But until that serious critic comes along,
Mr. Roscoe can certainly have the comfort of believing
that "if Achebe and Soyinka want to write in order to
change the world, Tutuola has other reasons."

And then Camara Laye. As recently as 1972 he was
saying in an interview:

> In showing the beauty of this culture, my novel
> testifies to its greatness. People who had not been
> aware that Africa had its own culture were able to
> grasp the significance of our past and our civilisation.
> I believe that this understanding is the most mean-
> ingful contribution of African literature.[14]

The distinguished and versatile Sierra Leonian, David-
son Abioseh Nicol—scientist, writer, and diplomat—
explaining why he wrote, said:

> . . . because I found that most of those who wrote
> about us seldom gave any nobility to their African
> characters unless they were savages or servants or
> facing impending destruction. I knew differently.

One could go on citing example after example of earnestness among African writers. But one final quotation

[13] Ibid, p. 92.
[14] Camara Laye, interviewed by J. Steven Rubin in *Africa Report*,
May 1972.

—from Kofi Awoonor, the fine Ghanaian poet, novelist, and essayist—should suffice:

> An African writer must be a person who has some kind of conception of the society in which he is living and the way he wants the society to go.

All this juvenile earnestness must give unbearable offense to mature people. Have we not heard, they may ask, what Americans say—that the place for sending messages is the Western Union? Perhaps we have; perhaps we haven't. But the plain fact is that we are *not* Americans. Americans have their vision; we have ours. We do not claim that ours is superior; we only ask to keep it. For, as my forefathers said, the firewood which a people have is adequate for the kind of cooking they do. To levy a charge of underdevelopment against African writers today may prove as misguided and uninformed as a similar dismissal of African art by visitors of an earlier age before the coming of Picasso. Those worthy men saw little good around them, only childlike and grotesque distortions. Frank Willett, in his excellent book, *African Art*, tells us of one such visitor to Benin in 1701, a certain David Nyendael, who on being taken to the royal gallery saw the objects as

> so wretchedly carved that it is hardly possible to distinguish whether they are most like men or beasts; notwithstanding which my guides were able to distinguish them into merchants, soldiers, wild-beast hunters, etc.[15]

[15] Frank Willett, *African Art*. New York: Praeger, 1971.

Most people today would be inclined to ascribe the wretchedness to Nyendael's own mind and taste rather than to the art of Benin. And yet, for me, his comment is almost saved by his acknowledgment, albeit grudging, of the very different perception of his guides, the real owners of the culture.

The colonialist critic, unwilling to accept the validity of sensibilities other than his own, has made particular point of dismissing the African novel. He has written lengthy articles to prove its non-existence largely on the grounds that it is a peculiarly Western genre, a fact which would interest us if our ambition was to write "Western" novels. But, in any case, did not the black people in America, deprived of their own musical instruments, take the trumpet and the trombone and blow them as they had never been blown before, as indeed they were not designed to be blown? And the result, was it not jazz? Is any one going to say that this was a loss to the world or that those first Negro slaves who began to play around with the discarded instruments of their masters should have played waltzes and fox trots and more Salvation Army hymn tunes? No! Let every people bring their gifts to the great festival of the world's cultural harvest and mankind will be all the richer for the variety and distinctiveness of the offerings.

Now, I spoke earlier on about an outsider whose wailing drowned the grief of the owners of the corpse. One last word to the owners. It is because our own critics have been somewhat hesitant in taking control of our literary criticism (sometimes—let's face it—for the good reason that they will not do the hard work that should equip them) that the task has fallen to others, some of whom (again we must admit) have been excellent and sensitive.

And yet most of what needs to be done can best be tackled by ourselves, the owners. If we fall back, can we complain that others are rushing forward? A man who does not lick his lips, can he blame the harmattan for drying them?

Let us emulate those men of Benin, ready to guide the curious visitor to the gallery of their art, willing to listen with politeness even to his hasty opinions, but careful, most careful, to concede nothing to him that might appear to undermine their own position within their heritage or compromise the integrity of their indigenous perception. For supposing the artists of Benin and of Congo and Angola had agreed with Nyendael in 1701 and abandoned their vision and begun to make their images in the style of developed Portugal, would they not have committed a grave disservice to Africa and ultimately to Europe and the rest of the world? Because they did not, it so happened that after the passage of two centuries other Europeans, more sensitive by far than Nyendael, looked at their work again and learned from it a new way to see the world.

1974

AFRICA AND HER WRITERS

Some time ago, in a very testy mood, I began a lecture with these words: *Art for art's sake is just another piece of deodorized dog shit.* Today, and particularly in these sublime and hallowed precincts,[1] I should be quite prepared to modify my language if not my opinion. In other words I will still insist that art is, and was always, in the service of man. Our ancestors created their myths and legends and told their stories for a human purpose (including, no doubt, the excitation of wonder and pure delight); they made their sculptures in wood and terra cotta, stone and bronze to serve the needs of their times. Their artists lived and moved and had their being in society and created their works for the good of that society.

I have just used the word *good*, which no decent man uses in polite society these days, and must hasten to explain. By *good* I do not mean moral uplift, although— —why not?—that would be part of it; I mean *good* in the sense in which God at the end of each day's work of put-

[1] Eliot House, Harvard University.

ting the world together saw that what He had made was good. Then, and only then, did He count it a day's job. *Good* in that sense does not mean pretty.

In the beginning art was good and useful; it always had its airy and magical qualities, of course; but even the magic was often intended to minister to a basic human need, to serve a down-to-earth necessity, as when the cavemen drew pictures on the rock of animals they hoped to kill in their next hunt!

But somewhere in the history of European civilization the idea that art should be accountable to no one, and needed to justify itself to nobody except itself, began to emerge. In the end it became a minor god and its devotees became priests urging all who are desirous to approach its altar to banish entirely from their hearts and minds such doubts and questions as *What use is this to me?* as the ultimate irreverence and profanation. Words like *use, purpose, value* are beneath the divine concerns of this Art, and so are we, the vulgarians craving the message and the morality. This Art exists independently of us, of all mankind. Man and his world may indeed pass away but not a jot from the laws of this Art.

Do I exaggerate? Perhaps a little, but not too much, I think. True, Edgar Allan Poe's famous lecture, "The Poetic Principle," may not now be the gospel it was to eariler generations, but the romantic idea of "the poem written solely for the poem's sake" still exerts a curious fascination on all kinds of people. I remember my surprise a few years ago at a conference of African writers when some obscure Rhodesian poet announced solemnly that a good poem writes itself. I very rarely wish writers ill, but that day I would have been happy if Shango had silenced that one with a nicely aimed thunderbolt and

given his ghost the eternal joy of watching new poems
surface onto his earthly notebook (or whatever he scrib-
bled his verses on).

Strangely enough (or perhaps not so strangely—perhaps we should rather say, appropriately) there is from
the same European mainspring another stream flowing
down the slopes on the other side of the hill, watering a
different soil and sustaining a different way of life. There,
on these other slopes, a poet is not a poet until the Writers'
Union tells him so. Between these two peoples, an
acrimonious argument rages. Each side hurls invective
over the hill into the other camp. *Monstrous philistines!*
Corrupt, decadent! So loud and bitter does the recrimination become that it is often difficult to believe that
these two peoples actually live on two slopes of the same
hill.

Once upon a time (according to my own adaptation
of a favorite Yoruba story), two farmers were working
their farms on either side of a road. As they worked
they made friendly conversation across the road. Then
Eshu, god of fate and lover of confusion, decided to upset the state of peace between them. A god with a sharp
and nimble imagination, he took his decision as quickly
as lightning. He rubbed one side of his body with white
chalk and the other side with charcoal and walked *up*
the road with considerable flourish between the farmers.
As soon as he passed beyond earshot the two men
jumped from their work at the same time. And one said:
"Did you notice that extraordinary white man who has
just gone up the road?" In the same breath the other
asked: "Did you see that incredible black man I have
just seen?" In no time at all the friendly questions turned
into a violent argument and quarrel, and finally into a

fight. As they fought they screamed: *He was white! He was black!* After they had belabored themselves to their hearts' content they went back to their farms and resumed their work in gloomy and hostile silence. But no sooner had they settled down than Eshu returned and passed with even greater flourish between them *down* the road. Immediately the two men sprang up again. And one said: "I am sorry, my good friend. You were right; the fellow is white." And in the same breath the other farmer was saying: "I do apologize for my blindness. The man is indeed black, just as you said." And in no time again the two were quarreling and then fighting. As they fought this time, they shouted: *I was wrong! No, I was wrong!*

The recrimination between capitalist and communist aesthetics in our time is, of course, comparable to the first act of the farmers' drama—the fight for the exclusive claim on righteousness and truth. Perhaps Eshu will return one day and pass again between them down the road and inaugurate the second act—the fight for self-abasement, for a monopoly on guilt.

As African writers emerge onto the world stage, they come under pressure to declare their stand. Now, I am not one for opposing an idea or a proposition simply on the grounds that it is "un-African"—a common enough ploy of obscurantist self-interest; thus a modern leader anxious to continue unchallenged his business of transforming public wealth into a dynastic fortune will often tell you that socialism (which, quite rightly, scares the daylights out of him) is un-African. We are not talking about *his* concern for Africanness. But there seems to me to be a genuine need for African writers to pause momentarily and consider whether anything in traditional

African aesthetics will fit their contemporary condition.
Let me give one example from Nigeria. Among the
Owerri Igbo there was a colorful ceremony called *mbari*,
a profound affirmation of the people's belief in the in-
divisibility of art and society. Mbari was performed at the
behest of the Earth goddess, Ala, the most powerful deity
in the Igbo pantheon, for she was not only the owner of
the soil but also controller of morality and creativity, artistic and biological. Every so many years Ala would in-
struct the community through her priest to prepare a
festival of images in her honor. That night the priest
would travel through the town, knocking on many doors
to announce to the various households whom of their
members Ala had chosen for the great work. These
chosen men and women then moved into seclusion in a
forest clearing and, under the instruction and guidance
of master artists and craftsmen, began to build a house
of images. The work might take a year or even two, but
as long as it lasted the workers were deemed to be hallowed and were protected from undue contact from, and
distraction by, the larger community.

The finished temple was architecturally simple—two
side walls and a back wall under a high thatched roof.
Steps ran the full width of the temple, ascending backward and upward almost to the roof. But in spite of the
simplicity of its structure, mbari was often a miracle of
artistic achievement—a breathtaking concourse of images
in bright, primary colors. Since the enterprise was in
honor of Ala, most of the work was done in her own material—simple molded earth. But the execution turned
this simple material into finished images of startling
power and diversity. The goddess had a central seat, usually with a child on her knee—a telling juxtaposition of

formidable (even, implacable) power and gentleness. Then there were other divinities; there were men, women, beasts, and birds, real or imaginary. Indeed the total life of the community was reflected—scenes of religious duty, of day-to-day tasks and diversions, and even of village scandal. The work completed, the village declared a feast and a holiday to honor the goddess of creativity and her children, the makers of images.

This brief and inadequate description can give no idea of the impact of mbari. Even the early Christian missionaries who were shocked by the frankness of some of the portrayals couldn't quite take their eyes off! But all I want to do is to point out one or two of the aesthetic ideas underlying mbari. First, the making of art is not the exclusive concern of a particular caste or secret society. Those young men and women whom the goddess chose for the re-enactment of creation were not "artists." They were ordinary members of society. Next time around, the choice would fall on other people. Of course, mere nomination would not turn every man into an artist—not even divine appointment could guarantee it. The discipline, instruction, and guidance of a master artist would be necessary. But not even a conjunction of those two conditions would insure infallibly the emergence of a new, exciting sculptor or painter. But mbari was not looking for that. It was looking for, and saying, something else: *There is no rigid barrier between makers of culture and its consumers. Art belongs to all and is a "function" of society.* When Senghor insists with such obvious conviction that every man is a poet, he is responding, I think, to this holistic concern of our traditional societies.

All this will, I dare say, sound like abominable heresy in the ears of mystique lovers. For their sake and their comfort, let me hasten to add that the idea of mbari does not deny the place or importance of the master with unusual talent and professional experience. Indeed it highlights such gift and competence by bringing them into play on the seminal potentialities of the community. Again, mbari does not deny the need for the creative artist to go apart from time to time so as to commune with himself, to look inwardly into his own soul. For when the festival is over, the villagers return to their normal lives again, and the master artists to their work and contemplation. But they can never after this experience, this creative communal enterprise, become strangers again to one another. And by logical and physical extension the greater community, which comes to the unveiling of the art and then receives its makers again into its normal life, becomes a beneficiary—indeed an active partaker—of this experience.

If one believes, as many seem to do in some so-called advanced cultures, that the hallmark of a true artist is the ability to ignore society (and paradoxically demand at the same time its attention and homage), then one must find the ruling concerns of mbari somewhat undramatic. Certainly no artist reared within the mbari culture could aspire to humiliate his community by hanging his canvas upside down in an exhibition and, withdrawing to a corner, watching viewers extol its many fine and hidden points with much nodding of the head and outpouring of sophisticated jargon. Could a more appalling relationship be imagined? And the artist who so blatantly dramatizes it has more to answer for than all those pathetic courtiers lost in admiration of the emperor's new clothes, desperately hiding in breathless garrulity the blankness of their vision. *They* are only victims of an irresponsible monarch's capriciousness. And quite rightly, it is not they but the emperor himself who suffers the ultimate humiliation.

There is, of course, a deep political implication to all this. The Igbo society from which the example of mbari was taken is notorious for its unbridled republicanism. A society that upholds and extols an opposing political system is likely to take a different cultural viewpoint. For example, the European aesthetic, which many African writers are accepting so uncritically, developed in a rigid oligarchical culture in which kings and their nobilities in the past cultivated a taste different from the common appetite. And since they monopolized the resources of the realm, they were able to buy over the artists in the society through diverse bribes, inducements, and patronage to minister to this taste. Thus over many generations a real differentiation occurred between aristocratic culture and the common culture. The latter, having no resources to develop itself, went into stagnation. Of course, there is such a thing as poetic justice, and in the fullness of time the high culture, living so long in rarefied reaches of the upper atmosphere, became sick. Somehow it sensed that unless it made contact again with the ground it would surely die. So it descended to the earthy, stagnant pool of the common culture and began to fish out between delicate beaks such healing tidbits as four-letter words.

Where does the African writer come in, in all this? Quite frankly he is confused. Sometimes—in a spasmodic seizure of confidence—he feels called upon to save Europe and the West by giving them Africa's peculiar gifts of healing, irrigating (in the words of Senghor) the Cartesian rationalism of Europe with black sensitivity through the gift of emotion. In his poem *Prayer to Masks* we are those very children called to sacrifice their lives like the poor man his last garment,

So that hereafter we may cry "hear" at the rebirth of the
    world being the leaven that the white flour needs.
For who else would teach rhythm to the world that has
    died of machines and cannons?
For who else should ejaculate the cry of joy that arouses
    the dead and the wise in a new dawn?
Say who else could return the memory of life to men with
    a torn hope?

And in his famous poem *New York* he tells that amazing metropolis what it must do to be saved.

New York! I say to you: New York let black blood flow
    into your blood
That it may rub the rust from your steel joints, like an oil
    of life
That it may give to your bridges the bend of buttocks and
    the suppleness of creepers.

The trouble is that personally I am not so sure of things to be able to claim for Africa such a messianic mission in the world. In the first place we would be hard put to it "in our present condition of health" (to use a common Nigerian cliché) to save anybody. In the second place the world may not wish to be saved, even if Africa had the power to.

In talking about the world here we really mean Europe and the West. But we have all got into the bad habit of regarding that slice of the globe as the whole thing. That

an African writer can so easily slip into this error is a
tribute to its hold upon the contemporary imagination.
For those of Europe and the West, such a habit if not entirely excusable is at least understandable. It can even
be amusing in a harmless way, as when, for example, a
game between Cincinnati and Minnesota is called the
World Series. But it ceases to be funny when it consigns
other continents and peoples into a kind of limbo; and it
begins to border on the grotesque when these continents
and peoples come to accept this view of the world and of
themselves.

Senghor's solicitude for the health and happiness of
Europe may indeed have a ring of quixotic adventure
about it, but at least it seems to be rooted in a positive
awareness of self. Not so some of the more recent—and
quite bizarre—fashions in African literature; for example,
the near-pathological eagerness to contract the sicknesses
of Europe in the horribly mistaken belief that our claim
to sophistication is improved thereby. I am talking, of
course, about the *human-condition* syndrome. Presumably European art and literature have every good reason
for going into a phase of despair. But ours does not. The
worst we can afford at present is disappointment. Perhaps
when we too have overreached ourselves in technical
achievement without spiritual growth, we shall be entitled to despair. Or, who knows? We may even learn
from the history of others and avoid that particular fate.
But whether we shall learn or not, there seems to me no
sense whatever in rushing out now, so prematurely, to an
assignation with a cruel destiny that will not be stirring
from her place for a long time yet.

There is a brilliant Ghanaian novelist, Ayi Kwei Armah,
who seems to me to be in grave danger of squandering

his enormous talents and energy in pursuit of the *human condition*. In an impressive first novel, *The Beautyful Ones Are Not Yet Born*, he gives us a striking parable of corruption in Ghana society and of one man who refuses to be contaminated by this filth.

It is a well-written book. Armah's command of language and imagery is of a very high order indeed. But it is a sick book. Sick, not with the sickness of Ghana, but with the sickness of the *human condition*. The hero, pale and passive and nameless—a creation in the best manner of existentialist writing—wanders through the story in an anguished half-sleep, neck-deep in despair and human excrement of which we see rather a lot in the book. Did I say he *refused* to be corrupted? He did not do anything as positive as refusing. He reminded me very strongly of that man and woman in a Jean-Paul Sartre novel who sit in anguished gloom in a restaurant and then in a sudden access of nihilistic energy seize table knives and stab their hands right through to the wood—to prove some very obscure point to each other. Except that Armah's hero would be quite incapable of suffering any seizure.

Ultimately the novel failed to convince me. And this was because Armah insists that this story is happening in Ghana and not in some modern, existentialist no man's land. He throws in quite a few realistic ingredients like Kwame Nkrumah to prove it. And that is a mistake. Just as the hero is nameless, so should everything else be; and Armah might have gotten away with a modern, "universal" story. Why did he not opt simply for that easy choice? I don't know. But I am going to be superstitious and say that Africa probably seized hold of his subconscious and insinuated there this deadly obligation—deadly, that is, to universalistic pretentions—to use his considerable talents in the service of a particular people and a particular place. Could it be that under this pressure Armah attempts to tell what Europe would call a modern story and Africa a moral fable, at the same time; to relate the fashions of European literature to the men and women of Ghana? He tried very hard. But his Ghana is unrecognizable. This aura of cosmic sorrow and despair is as foreign and un-usable as those monstrous machines Nkrumah was said to have imported from Eastern European countries. Said, that is, by critics like Armah.

True, Ghana was sick. And what country is not? But everybody has his own brand of ailment. Ayi Kwei Ar-mah imposes so much foreign metaphor on the sickness of Ghana that it ceases to be true. And finally, the sugges-tion (albeit existentially tentative) of the hero's personal justification without faith nor works is grossly inadequate in a society where even a lunatic walking stark naked through the highways of Accra has an extended family somewhere suffering vicarious shame.

Armah is clearly an alienated writer, a modern writer complete with all the symptoms. Unfortunately Ghana is not a modern existentialist country. It is just a Western African state struggling to become a nation. So there is enormous distance between Armah and Ghana. There is something scornful, cold and remote about Armah's ob-session with the filth of Ghana:

Left-hand fingers in their careless journey from a hasty anus sliding all the way up the banister as their owners made the return trip from the lavatory down-stairs to the offices above. Right-hand fingers still dripping with the after-piss and the stale sweat from fat crotches. The callused palms of messengers after

they had blown their clogged noses reaching for a
convenient place to leave the well-rubbed moisture.
Afternoon hands not entirely licked clean of palm
soup and remnants of *kenkey*. . . .

You have to go to certain European writers on Africa
to find something of the same attitude and icy distance:

Fada is the ordinary native town of the Western
Sudan. It has no beauty, convenience or health. It is
a dwelling place at one stage from the rabbit warren
and the badger burrow; and not so cleanly kept as
the latter. It is . . . built on its own rubbish heaps,
without charm even of antiquity. Its squalor and its
stinks are all new. . . . All its mud walls are eaten
as if by small-pox. . . . Its people would not know
the change if time jumped back fifty thousand years.
They live like mice or rats in a palace floor; all the
magnificence and variety of the arts, the learning and
the battles of civilisation go on over their heads and
they do not even imagine them.

That is from Joyce Cary's famous novel, *Mister Johnson*, "the best novel ever written about Africa" according
to *Time* magazine. Joyce Cary was an alien writing about
Africa; Ayi Kwei Armah is the alienated native. It seems
that to achieve the modern alienated stance an African
writer will end up writing like some white District Officer.
Armah is quoted somewhere as saying that he is not an
African writer but just a writer. Some other writers (and
friends of mine, all) have said the same thing. It is a senti-
ment guaranteed to win applause in Western circles. But
it is a statement of defeat. A man is never more defeated

than when he is running away from himself. When Pablo Neruda received the Nobel Prize for Literature in 1971, he said:

I belong to all the people of Latin America, a little of whose soul I have tried to interpret.

I wonder what an African writer would have said. Perhaps "I belong to the universe, all of whose soul I have successfully interpreted."

I know the source of our problem, of course. *Anxiety.* Africa has had such a fate in the world that the very adjective *African* can still call up hideous fears of rejection. Better then to cut all links with this homeland, this liability, and become in one giant leap the universal man. Indeed, I understand the anxiety. But running away from myself seems to me a very inadequate way of dealing with an anxiety. And if writers should opt for such escapism, who is to meet the challenge?

Sometimes this problem appears in almost comical forms. A young Nigerian poet living and teaching in New York sent me in Nigeria a poem for the literary magazine I edit. It was a good poem but in one of his lines he used a plural Italian word as if it were singular. And there was no reason I could see for invoking poetic license. So I made the slightest alteration imaginable in the verb to correct this needless error. The bright, young poet, instead of thanking me, wrote an angry and devastating letter in which he accused me of being a grammarian. I didn't mind that, really; it was a new kind of accusation. But in his final crushing statement he contrasted the linguistic conservatism of those who live in the outposts of empire with the imaginative freedom of the dwellers of the metropolis.

At first I thought of replying but in the end decided it was a waste of my time. If I had replied, I would have agreed with him about our respective locations, but would have gone on to remind him that the outposts had always borne the historic role of defending the empire from the constant threat of the barbarian hordes; and so needed always to be awake and alert, unlike the easygoing, soft-living metropolis.

But jokes apart, this incident is really a neat parable of the predicament of the African writer in search of universality. He has been misled into thinking that the metropolis belongs to him. Well, not yet. For him there is still the inescapable grammar of values to straighten out, the confused vocabulary of fledgling polities. Ease and carelessness in our circumstance will only cause a total breakdown of communications.

But you might say: What does it really matter? A man could have the wrongest ideas and yet write good poems and good novels, while another with impeccable notions writes terrible books. This may be true. Certainly those who will write bad books will probably write bad books whatever ideas they may hold. It is the good, or the potentially good, writer who should interest us. And for him I will sooner risk good ideas than bad. I don't believe he will come to much harm by asking himself a few pointed questions.

The late Christopher Okigbo was perhaps a good example of an artist who sometimes had, and expressed, confusing ideas while producing immaculate poetry. He was, in the view of many, Africa's finest poet of our time. For while other poets wrote good poems, Okigbo con-

jured up for us an amazing, haunting poetic firmament of
a wild and violent beauty. Well, Christopher Okigbo once
said that he wrote his poems only for other poets: thus
putting himself not just beyond the African pale but in a
position that would have shocked the great English Romantic poet who defined himself as a man writing for
men. On another occasion Okigbo said: "There is no
African literature. There is good writing and bad writing
—that's all." But quite quickly we are led to suspect that
this was all bluff. For when Okigbo was asked why he
turned to poetry, he said:

> The turning point came in 1958 when I found myself
> wanting to know myself better, and I had to turn and
> look at myself from inside. . . . And when I talk of
> looking inward to myself, I mean turning inward to
> examine myselves. This, of course, takes account of
> ancestors. . . . Because I do not exist apart from my
> ancestors.

And then, as though to spell it out clearly that ancestors
does not mean some general psychological or genetic
principle, Okigbo tells us specifically that he is the reincarnation of his maternal grandfather, a priest in the
shrine of the Earth goddess. In fact, poetry becomes for
him an anguished journey back from alienation to re-
sumption of ritual and priestly functions. His voice becomes the voice of the sunbird of Igbo mythology,
mysterious and ominous.

But it was not a simple choice or an easy return journey
for Okigbo to make, for he never underrated his indebt-
edness to the rest of the world. He brought into his poetry
all the heirlooms of his multiple heritage; he ranged with

ease through Rome and Greece and Babylon, through the
rites of Judaism and Catholicism, through European and
Bengali literatures, through modern music and painting.
But at least one perceptive Nigerian critic has argued
that Okigbo's true voice only came to him in his last se-
quence of poems, *Path of Thunder,* when he had finally
and decisively opted for an African inspiration. This
opinion may be contested, though I think it has substantial
merit. The trouble is that Okigbo is such a bewitching
poet, able to cast such a powerful spell that, whatever he
cares to say or sing, we stand breathless at the sheer
beauty and grace of his sound and imagery. Yet there
is that undeniable fire in his last poems which was something new. It was as though the goddess he sought in his
poetic journey through so many alien landscapes, and
ultimately found at home, had given him this new thunder. Unfortunately, when he was killed in 1967 he left us
only that little, tantalizing hint of the new self he had
found. But perhaps he will be reincarnated in other poets
and sing for us again like his sunbird whose imperishable
song survived the ravages of the eagles.

1973

LANGUAGE AND THE DESTINY
OF MAN

In his long evolutionary history man has scored few
greater successes than his creation of human society. For
it was on that primeval achievement that he has built
those special qualities of mind and of behavior which,
in his own view at least, separate him from lower forms
of life. If we sometimes tend to overlook this fact, it is
only because we have lived so long under the protective
ambiance of society that we have come to take its benefits
for granted. Which, in a way, might be called the ultimate tribute; rather like the unspoken worship and
thanksgiving which a man renders with every breath he
draws. If it were different, we would not be men but
angels, incapable of boredom.

Unquestionably, language was crucial to the creation of
society. There is no way in which human society could
exist without speech. By society we do not, of course,
mean the mechanical and mindless association of the bee-
hive or the anthill which employs certain rudimentary

forms of communication to achieve an unvarying, instinctual purpose, but a community where man "doomed to be free"—to use Joyce Cary's remarkable phrase—is yet able to challenge that peculiar and perilous destiny with an even chance of wresting from it a purposeful, creative existence.

Speech too, like society itself, seems so natural that we rarely give much thought to it or contemplate man's circumstance before its invention. But we know that language is not inherent in man—the capacity for language, yes; but not language. Therefore there must have been a time in the very distant past when our ancestors did not have it. Let us imagine a very simple incident in those days. A man strays into a rock shelter without knowing that another is there finishing a meal in the dark interior. The first hint our newcomer gets of this fact is a loose rock hurled at his head. In a different kind of situation, which we shall call (with all kinds of guilty reservations) *human*, that confrontation might have been resolved less destructively by the simple question: *What do you want?* or even an angry: *Get out of here!*

Nobody is, of course, going to be so naïve as to claim for language the power to dispose of all, or even most, violence. After all man is not less violent than other animals, but more—apparently the only one which consistently visits violence on its own kind. Yet in spite of this (or perhaps because of it) one does have a feeling that without language we should have long been extinct.

Many people, following the fascinating progress of Dr. L. S. B. Leaky's famous excavations in the Olduvai Gorge in eastern Africa in the 1950s, were shocked by his claim that the so-called "pre-Zinjanthropus" child, the discovery of whose remains stirred many hearts and was one of the high lights of modern paleontology, was probably murdered, aged about twelve. Another excavator, Professor Raymond Dart, working farther south, has collected much similar evidence of homicide in the caves of Transvaal.[1] But we should not have been surprised or shocked unless we had overlooked the psychological probability of the murder outside the Garden of Eden.

Let us take a second and quite different kind of example. Let us imagine an infant crying. Its mother assumes that it is hungry and offers it food; but it refuses to eat and goes on crying. Is it wet? Does it have pain? If so, where? Has an ant crawled into its dress and bitten it? Does it want to sleep? etc., etc. Thus the mother, especially if she lacks experience (as more and more mothers tend to do), will grope from one impulse to another, from one possibility to its opposite until she stumbles on the right one. Meanwhile the child suffers distress, and she, mental anguish. In other words, because of a child's inadequate vocabulary, even its simplest needs cannot be quickly known and satisfied. From which rather silly example we can see, I hope, the value of language in facilitating the affairs and transactions of society by enabling its members to pass on their message quickly and exactly.

In small close-knit societies, such as we often call primitive, the importance of language is seen in pristine clarity. For instance, in the creation myth of the Hebrews,

[1] Sonia Cole, *The Prehistory of East Africa*. London: Wedenfeld & Nicolson.

God made the world by word of mouth; and in the Christian myth, as recorded in St. John's Gospel, the Word became God himself.

African societies in the past held similar notions about language and the potency of words. Writing about Igbo society in Nigeria, Igwe and Green had this to say:

> a speaker who could use language effectively and had a good command of idioms and proverbs was respected by his fellows and was often a leader in the community.[2]

From another part of Africa a Kenyan, Mugo Gatheru, in his autobiographical book gives even stronger testimony from his people:

> among the Kikuyu those who speak well have always been honoured, and the very word *chief* means *good talker*.[3]

There is a remarkable creation myth among the Wapangwa people of Tanzania which begins thus:

> The sky was large, white, and very clear. It was empty; there were no stars and no moon; only a tree stood in the air and there was wind. This tree fed on the atmosphere and ants lived on it. Wind, tree, ants, and atmosphere were controlled by the power of the Word, but the Word was not something that could be

[2] G. E. Igwe & M. M. Green, *Igbo Language Course*. London: Oxford University Press.

[3] Mugo Gatheru, *A Child of Two Worlds*. London: Heinemann Educational Books, p. 40.

seen. It was a force that enabled one thing to create
another.[4]

But although contemporary societies in Africa and elsewhere have moved away from beliefs and attitudes which
had invested language with such ritual qualities, we can
still find remains of the old dignity in certain places and
circumstances. In his famous autobiography, Camara
Laye records the survival of such an attitude in the Guinea
of his boyhood: the strong impression that the traditional
village could make on the visitor from the town.

> In everything, I noticed a kind of dignity which was
> often lacking in town life. . . . And if their minds
> seemed to work slower in the country, that was be-
> cause they always spoke only after due reflection,
> and because speech itself was a most serious matter.[5]

And finally, from a totally different environment, these
lines of a traditional Eskimo poem, *Magic Words,* from
Jerome Rothenberg's excellent anthology, *Shaking the
Pumpkin:*

> That was the time when words were like magic
> The human mind had mysterious powers.
> A word spoken by chance
> might have strange consequences.
> It would suddenly come alive
> and what people wanted to happen could happen—
> all you had to do was say it.[6]

[4] Ulli Beier, ed., *The Origin of Life and Death.* London: Heinemann.
[5] Camara Laye, *The African Child.* London and Glasgow: Fontana,
p. 53.
[6] Jerome Rothenberg, ed., *Shaking the Pumpkin.* New York: Doubleday.

In small and self-sufficient societies such as gave birth to these myths, the integrity of language is safeguarded by the fact that what goes on in the community can easily be ascertained, understood, and evaluated by all. The line between truth and falsehood thus tends to be sharp, and when a man addresses his fellows, they know already what kind of person he is, whether (as Igbo people would put it) he is one with whose words something can be done; or else who, if he tells you to stand, you know you must immediately flee!

But as society becomes larger and more complex, we find that we can no longer be in command of all the facts but are obliged to take a good deal of what we hear on trust. We delegate to others the power to take certain decisions on our behalf, and they may not always be people we know or can vouch for. I shall return shortly to a consideration of this phenomenon. But first I shall consider a different, though related, problem—the pressure to which language is subjected by the mere fact that it can never change fast enough to deal with every new factor in the ever-increasing complexity of the life of the community, to say nothing of the private perceptions and idiosyncracies of particular speakers. T. S. Eliot comes readily to mind with those memorable lines in which he suggests to us the constant struggle, frustration, and anguish which this situation imposes on a poet:

> . . . Trying to learn to use words, and every attempt
> Is a wholly new start and a different kind of failure
> Because one has only learnt to get the better of words
> For the thing one no longer has to say, or the way in
>   which
> One is no longer disposed to say it. . . .

Of course one might wonder whether this problem was a real one for ordinary people like ourselves or a peculiar species of self-flagellation by a high-strung devotee seeking through torment to become worthy of his deity. For, as in these well-known lines, Eliot's celebration of his ideal can sometimes assume accents of holy intoxication:

> And every phrase
> And sentence that is right (where every word is at home,
> Taking its place to support the others
> The word neither diffident nor ostentatious,
> An easy commerce of the old and the new,
> The common word exact without vulgarity,
> The formal word precise but not pedantic,
> The complete consort dancing together)
> Every phrase and every sentence is an end and a begin-
>   ning,
> Every poem an epitaph.

This curious mix of high purpose and carnival jollity may leave us a little puzzled, but there is no doubt whatever about Eliot's concern and solicitude for the integrity of words. And let us not imagine, even the most prosaic among us, that this concern and the stringent practice Eliot advocates are appropriate only to poets. For we all stand to lose when language is debased, just as every one of us is affected when the nation's currency is devalued; not just the Secretary of the Treasury, or controllers of our banks.

Talking about secretaries of the Treasury and devaluation, there was an amusing quotation by Professor Douglas Bush in an essay entitled "Polluting Our Lan-

guages" in the Spring 1972 issue of *The American Scholar*.
The Secretary of the Treasury, John Connally, had said:
"In the early sixties we were strong; we were virulent."
Clearly that was only a slip, albeit of a kind that might
interest Freudians. But it might not be entirely unfair to
see a tendency to devaluation inherent in certain occupa-
tions!

We must now turn from considering the necessary struggle with language arising, as it were, from its very nature
and the nature of the society it serves to the more ominous
threat to its integrity brought about neither by its innate
inadequacy nor yet by the incompetence and carelessness
of its ordinary users, but rather engineered deliberately
by those who will manipulate words for their own ends.
It has long been known that language, like any other human invention, can be abused, can be turned from its
original purpose into something useless or even deadly.
George Orwell, who was very much concerned in his writings with this modern menace, reminds us that language
can be used not only for expressing thought but for con-
cealing thought or even preventing thought.[7] I guess we
are all too familiar with this—from the mild assault of the
sales pitch which exhorts you: "Be progressive! Use ABC
toothpaste!" or invites you to a *saving spree* in a depart-
ment store; through the mystifications of learned people
jealously guarding the precincts of their secret societies
with such shibboleths as: "Bilateral mastectomy was performed" instead of "Both breasts were removed"[8]; to

[7] George Orwell, "Politics and the English Language," in *Essays*. New
York: Doubleday.
[8] Dr. F. Nwako, "Disorders in Medical Education," in *Nsukkascope*,
1972.

the politician who employs government prose to keep you in the dark about affairs on which your life or the lives of your children may depend, or the official statistician who assures you that crime rates "are increasing at a decreasing rate of increase." I shall not waste your time about this well-known fact of modern life. But let me round off this aspect of the matter by quoting a little of the comment made by W. H. Auden in an interview published by the New York *Times* (October 19, 1971):

> As a poet—not as a citizen—there is only one political duty, and that is to defend one's language from corruption. And that is particularly serious now. It's being so quickly corrupted. When it is corrupted, people lose faith in what they hear, and this leads to violence.

And leads also full circle to the cave-man situation with which we began. And the heart of my purpose is to suggest that our remote ancestors who made and preserved language for us, who, you might say, crossed the first threshold from bestiality to humanness, left us also adequate warning, wrapped in symbols, against its misuse.

Every people has a body of myths or sacred tales received from its antiquity. They are supernatural stories which man created to explain the problems and mysteries of life and death—his attempt to make sense of the bewildering complexity of existence. There is a proud, nomadic people, the Fulani, who inhabit the northern savannahs of Western Africa from Cameroun and Nigeria westward to Mali and Senegal. They are very much attached to their

cattle, whose milk is their staff of life. Here is a Fulani
myth of creation from Mali:

At the beginning there was a huge drop of milk.
Then Doondari came and he created the stone.
Then the stone created iron;
And iron created fire;
And fire created water;
And water created air.

Then Doondari descended the second time.
And he took the five elements,
And he shaped them into man.
But man was proud.
Then Doondari created blindness and blindness defeated
    man.
But when blindness became too proud,
Doondari created sleep, and sleep defeated blindness;
But when sleep became too proud,
Doondari created worry, and worry defeated sleep;
But when worry became too proud,
Doondari created death, and death defeated worry.

But when death became too proud,
Doondari descended for the third time,
And he came as Gueno, the eternal one
And Gueno defeated death.[9]

You notice, don't you, how in the second section of that
poem, after the creation of man, we have that phrase

[9] Ulli Beier, op. cit.

became too proud coming back again and again like the recurrence of a dominant beat in rhythmic music? Clearly the makers of that myth intended us not to miss it. So it was at the very heart of their purpose. MAN IS DESTROYED BY PRIDE. It is said over and over again; it is shouted like a message across vast distances until the man at the other end of the savannah has definitely got it, despite the noise of rushing winds. Or if you prefer a modern metaphor, it is like making a long-distance call when the line is faulty or in bad weather. You shout your message and repeat it again and again just to make sure.

Claude Levi-Strauss, the French structural anthropologist, has indeed sought to explain the repetitive factor in myth in this way, relating it to general information theory. Our forefathers and ancestors are seen in the role of *senders* of the message, and we, the novices of society, as *receivers*.[10] The ancestors are sending us signals from the long history and experience of by-gone days about the meaning of life, the qualities we should cultivate, and the values that are important. Because they are so far away and because we are surrounded by the tumult and distractions of daily life, they have to shout and repeat themselves not only in phrase after phrase but also in myth after myth, varying the form slightly now and again until the central message goes home.

If this interpretation is right, then the Fulani myth of creation delivers not only a particular message on the danger of pride but also exemplifies beautifully the general intention and purpose of myths. Let us now look at

10 Edmund Leach, *Levi-Strauss*. London: Fontana/Collins.

another short myth from the Igbo people in Nigeria which
bears more directly on the question of language:

> When death first entered the world, men sent a mes-
> senger to Chuku, asking him whether the dead could
> not be restored to life and sent back to their old
> homes. They chose the dog as their messenger.
>
> The dog, however, did not go straight to Chuku, and
> dallied on the way. The toad had overheard the
> message, and as he wished to punish mankind, he
> overtook the dog and reached Chuku first. He said
> he had been sent by men to say that after death they
> had no desire at all to return to the world. Chuku
> declared that he would respect their wishes, and
> when the dog arrived with the true message he re-
> fused to alter his decision.
>
> Thus although a human being may be born again,
> he cannot return with the same body and the same
> personality.[11]

It has been pointed out that there are more than seven
hundred different versions of this myth all over Africa.
Thus the element of repetition, which we have seen in
the form of a phrase recurring in time within one myth,
takes on the formidable power of spatial dispersion across
a continent. Clearly the ancestral senders regard this particular signal as of desperate importance, hence its
ubiquity and the profuse variations of its theme. Sometimes the messenger is the dog; sometimes, the chameleon
or the lizard or some other animal. In some versions the

[11] Ulli Beier, op. cit.

message is garbled through the incompetence of the messenger, or through his calculated malice against men. In others man in his impatience sends a second messenger to God who in anger withdraws the gift of immortality. But whatever variations in the detail, the dominant theme remains: Men send a messenger to their Creator with a plea for immortality and He is disposed to grant their request. But something goes wrong with the message at the last moment. And this bounty which mankind has all but held in its grasp, this monumental gift that would have made man more like the gods, is snatched from him forever. And he knows that there is a way to hell even from the gates of heaven!

This, to my mind, is the great myth about language and the destiny of man. Its lesson should be clear to all. It is as though the ancestors, who made language and knew from what bestiality its use rescued them, are saying to us: Beware of interfering with its purpose! For when language is seriously interfered with, when it is disjoined from truth, be it from mere incompetence or worse, from malice, horrors can descend again on mankind.

Dartmouth College

June 1972

WHAT DO AFRICAN INTELLECTUALS READ?

The temptation is indeed strong to answer that question in one word: nothing. But such an answer would be too simplistic—neither wholly true nor very helpful. A satisfactory answer has to be a little more complex, has to be hedged in here and there by exceptions, qualifications, even excuses.

Surely, the African intellectual reads *Newsweek* and *Time* magazines and one or two local papers as well. And it is conceivable that he might even find time once in a while to dip into that decorative set of encyclopedias one sees more and more these days adorning the sitting rooms of the intellectual elite and their emulators, although I doubt it.

Time is a serious handicap. In the major urban areas where the intellectuals generally live with other elite groups (political, business, military, etc.) time tends to be shorter and shorter. After the day's work and siesta and perhaps, for the very conscientious, another hour or

two in the office, there is television before the rounds of
cocktail and dinner parties that might go on into the small
hours. As the number of our intellectuals is still relatively
small, they all tend to belong to the same tiny, highly
sought-after group and to be drawn into the same cycle
of time-consuming high life.

But there are other limiting factors besides time. The
habit of reading itself is clearly the most important, for if
it were strongly developed in our intellectuals, some of
them at least would find the time. But the habit is simply
not there.

In 1958, or 1959, I did a little crude research in a small
British Council library at Enugu, where I lived at the time.
From that little exercise, I proved to my own statistical
satisfaction what I had always known instinctively. I
discovered that the European residents of Enugu read fiction, poetry, drama, etc. while Africans read history, economics, mathematics, etc. My research was easy enough
because the library had the interesting, and convenient
(if somewhat unconventional), system of recording in
pink or black on the borrowing card according to the color
of the borrower. (I hasten to add that no racism was ever
intended: the system was developed out of a genuine
curiosity to ascertain the reading habits of the two communities.)

It was clear that the Africans who went to that library
did not go in search of literary pleasure. They were concerned mostly with one or other of the many external
examinations of London University or the City and
Guilds.

In the last few months I was told separately by two
university professors of about my own generation (one
from Ibadan, Nigeria, and the other from Lusaka, Zam-

bia) that they never had time to read fiction. The one
from Lusaka was gracious enough to add "except your
books." The other, a historian, made no such concessions;
the farthest he was prepared to wander from history was
to biographies.

When these two professors were at school fifteen or
twenty years ago, they probably never read anything that
wasn't a textbook. If they were offered literature in their
Cambridge School Certificate, then they probably read a
couple of novels like *Pride and Prejudice, Wuthering
Heights, Far Away and Long Ago,* one Shakespeare play,
most likely *Julius Caesar* or *Romeo and Juliet,* and that
would be all. In their class there might be a boy or
two who had a special flair for literature and would
pick up on their own some Peter Cheyney or Agatha
Christie, but more likely Marie Corelli and Bertha Clay.

So high was the admiration for Marie Corelli that in a
little book just published in Nigeria, by someone who was
probably at school at the same time as my two professors,
she is numbered among the world's superwomen, in the
company of Joan of Arc and Mary Magdalene.

Such was the literary background of today's African
intellectuals. Many of them are eminent in their various
academic disciplines and professions and seem none the
worse for their shaky literary beginnings (and are certainly unaware of Fowler's conceit about an illiterate man
being not simply one who cannot read and write but one
who is unacquainted with good literature). So much for
the present. What is the augury for the future? Will the
intellectuals of tomorrow (who are at school today) read
more, or is the book, already pronounced dead by some in
the West, going to be stillborn in Africa?

The most hopeful sign is that books and reading are so

much more in the air today. Even those who confess to
not reading still find the need to make the confession.
One might almost talk of a literary ambiance. Present-
day schoolchildren are much more aware of literature
than was generally the case in my own school days. And
I mean literature as a living phenomenon. So many of
them today are not just passively aware; they want to
write and *are* writing.

Two factors give them an advantage over my own generation. There are more books around and more libraries;
and there are books with a familiar ring and background.

The availability of books is of crucial importance in
creating both committed readers and future writers. The
number of young people who are writing or wanting to
write in Africa today must be immense. I get letters all
the time from East and West Africa from such people.
Even as I write now I have a batch of rather impressive
poems from an unemployed young man in Lagos; I have
before me a letter from a soldier in some remote part of
Nigeria who says he has completed a novel and would
like me to see it; and I have on my table about twenty
manuscripts of novels that managed somehow to pene-
trate my recent antimanuscript barricade.

When I was a boy, things were rather different. Books
were rare indeed. I remember the very strong impression
made on me by the rows and rows of books in my school
library when I first got there in 1944. I was, of course,
most fortunate in gaining admission to a government college, one of those rare schools which the colonial administration built and endowed lavishly, for obscure reasons
of its own. Cricket was played zealously and, in one of
them at least, Eton Fives. But their most valuable asset
was books. It is no doubt significant that, besides myself,

almost all of the first generation of Nigerian writers had gone to one of the four or five government colleges: T. M. Aluko, Cyprian Ekwensi, Gabriel Okara, Wole Soyinka, J. P. Clark, Christopher Okigbo, V. C. Ike, Nkem Nwankwo, Elechi Amadi.

By contrast, the vast majority of schools had inadequate libraries or none at all. I was not to know fully what advantage we had had until I went years later to teach in one of the so-called private schools in my district and discovered that the school "library" consisted of a dusty cupboard containing one copy of the Holy Bible, five pamphlets entitled *The Adventures of Tarzan*, and one copy of a popular novel called *The Sorrows of Satan*.

Things have greatly improved. Books are today much more widely available in schools and public libraries. And what is more, the young reader can read something from African literature. We never had that. In our time, literature was just another marvel that came with all the other wondrous things of civilization, like motor cars and airplanes, from far away. They had very little to do with us, or rather we had very little to do with them, except in the role of wide-eyed consumers. Today, in the realm of literature at least, such inhibiting non-identification is already a thing of the past.

The inheritor of that impressive set of encyclopedias acquired today for prestige on hire-purchase may actually come to use it.

Let me end on a paradoxical note. If the present-day intellectuals in Africa have read so little from the literature of the West, with which they had such close dealings and by which their destiny was so largely shaped, how has this affected their picture of the West and through the West their view of the world? The African intellectual's knowledge of the West (and he knows a lot more about the West than the Western intellectual knows about Africa) comes to him not from literature but from personal contact. African intellectuals are among the most widely traveled in the world today. Just as they are in high demand at embassy parties in their national capitals, so are they assiduously courted with foreign scholarships, fellowships, travel grants, and all kinds of business and professional junketing abroad. And many of them in any case had their higher education in Europe and North America; and those who studied in the new African universities were likely to have been taught by teachers from the West.

These firsthand contacts are bound to decrease in significance as the over-all population of African intellectuals increases and as African universities become more and more Africanized. As this trend continues, African intellectuals will become more generally ignorant of Europeans and Americans even as these are today ignorant of Africans. Therefore we may speculate about a future in which the African intellectual will come to rely for his knowledge of the West on myths and stock images from that kind of popular literature which most easily crosses cultural frontiers. But let us hope that this may be somewhat offset by a greater knowledge of himself, and of Africa, from his own literature.

1972

THE NOVELIST AS TEACHER

Writing of the kind I do is relatively new in my part of the world and it is too soon to try and describe in detail the complex of relationships between us and our readers. However, I think I can safely deal with one aspect of these relationships which is rarely mentioned. Because of our largely European education, our writers may be pardoned if they begin by thinking that the relationship between European writers and their audience will automatically reproduce itself in Africa. We have learned from Europe that a writer or an artist lives on the fringe of society—wearing a beard and a peculiar dress and generally behaving in a strange, unpredictable way. He is in revolt against society, which in turn looks on him with suspicion if not hostility. The last thing society would dream of doing is to put him in charge of anything.

All that is well known, which is why some of us seem too eager for our society to treat us with the same hostility or even behave as though it already does. But I am not interested now in what writers expect of society; that is generally contained in their books, or should be. What is not so well documented is what society expects of its writers.

I am assuming, of course, that our writer and his society live in the same place. I realize that a lot has been made of the allegation that African writers have to write for European and American readers because African readers, where they exist at all, are only interested in reading textbooks. I don't know if African writers always have a foreign audience in mind. What I do know is that they don't have to. At least I know that I don't have to. Last year the pattern of sales of *Things Fall Apart* in the cheap paperback edition was as follows: about 800 copies in Britain; 20,000 in Nigeria; and about 2,500 in all other places. The same pattern was true also of *No Longer at Ease*.

Most of my readers are young. They are either in school or college or have only recently left. And many of them look at me as a kind of teacher. Only the other day I received this letter from Northern Nigeria:

Dear C. Achebe,

I do not usually write to authors, no matter how interesting their work is, but I feel I must tell you how much I enjoyed your editions of *Things Fall Apart* and *No Longer at Ease*. I look forward to reading your new edition *Arrow of God*. Your novels serve as advice to us young. I trust that you will continue to produce as many of this type of book. With friendly greetings and best wishes.

Yours sincerely,

I. Buba Yero Mafindi

It is quite clear what this particular reader expects of me. Nor is there much doubt about another reader in Ghana who wrote me a rather pathetic letter to say that I had neglected to include questions and answers at the end of *Things Fall Apart* and could I make these available to him to insure his success at next year's school certificate examinations. This is what I would call in Nigerian pidgin "a how-for-do" reader and I hope there are not very many like him. But also in Ghana I met a young woman teacher who immediately took me to task for not making the hero of my *No Longer at Ease* marry the girl he is in love with. I made the kind of vague noises I usually make whenever a wise critic comes along to tell me I should have written a different book to the one I wrote. But my woman teacher was not going to be shaken off so easily. She was in deadly earnest. Did I know, she said, that there were many women in the kind of situation I had described and that I could have served them well if I had shown that it was possible to find one man with enough guts to go against custom?

I don't agree, of course. But this young woman spoke with so much feeling that I couldn't help being a little uneasy at the accusation (for it was indeed a serious accusation) that I had squandered a rare opportunity for education on a whimsical and frivolous exercise. It is important to say at this point that no self-respecting writer will take dictation from his audience. He must remain free to disagree with his society and go into rebellion against it if need be. But I am for choosing my cause very carefully. Why should I start waging war as a Nigerian newspaper editor was doing the other day on the "soulless efficiency" of Europe's industrial and technological civili-

zation when the very thing my society needs may well
be a little technical efficiency?

My thinking on the peculiar needs of different societies
was sharpened when not long ago I heard an English
pop song, which I think was entitled "I Ain't Gonna Wash
for a Week." At first I wondered why it should occur to
anyone to take such a vow when there were so many much
more worthwhile resolutions to make. But later it dawned
on me that this singer belonged to the same culture which,
in an earlier age of self-satisfaction, had blasphemed and
said that cleanliness was next to godliness. So I saw him
in a new light—as a kind of divine administrator of venge-
ance. I make bold to say, however, that his particular offices would not be required in my society because we did
not commit the sin of turning hygiene into a god.

Needless to say, we do have our own sins and blasphe-
mies recorded against our name. If I were God, I would
regard as the very worst our acceptance—for whatever
reason—of racial inferiority. It is too late in the day to get
worked up about it or to blame others, much as they may
deserve such blame and condemnation. What we need to
do is to look back and try to find out where we went
wrong, where the rain began to beat us.

Let me give one or two examples of the result of the
disaster brought upon the African psyche in the period of
subjection to alien races. I remember the shock felt by
Christians of my father's generation in my village in the
early forties when, for the first time, the local girls' school
performed Nigerian dances at the anniversary of the coming of the gospel. Hitherto they had always put on something Christian and civilized which I believe was called
the Maypole dance. In those days—when I was growing
up—I also remember that it was only the poor benighted

heathen who had any use for our local handicraft, e.g., our pottery. Christians and the well-to-do (and they were usually the same people) displayed their tins and other metalware. We never carried waterpots to the stream. I had a small cylindrical biscuit tin suitable to my years, while the older members of our household carried four-gallon kerosene tins.

Today, things have changed a lot, but it would be foolish to pretend that we have fully recovered from the traumatic effects of our first confrontation with Europe. Three or four weeks ago, my wife, who teaches English in a boys' school, asked a pupil why he wrote about winter when he meant the harmattan. He said the other boys would call him a bushman if he did such a thing! Now, you wouldn't have thought, would you, that there was something shameful in your weather? But apparently we do. How can this great blasphemy be purged? I think it is part of my business as a writer to teach that boy that there is nothing disgraceful about the African weather, that the palm tree is a fit subject for poetry.

Here then is an adequate revolution for me to espouse —to help my society regain belief in itself and put away the complexes of the years of denigration and self-abasement. And it is essentially a question of education, in the best sense of that word. Here, I think, my aims and the deepest aspirations of my society meet. For no thinking African can escape the pain of the wound in our soul. You have all heard of the African personality, of African democracy, of the African way to socialism, of negritude, and so on. They are all props we have fashioned at different times to help us get on our feet again. Once we are up, we shan't need any of them any more. But for the moment it is in the nature of things that we may need to counter racism with what Jean-Paul Sartre has called an antiracist racism, to announce not just that we are as good as the next man but that we are much better.

The writer cannot expect to be excused from the task of re-education and regeneration that must be done. In fact he should march right in front. For he is after all—as Ezekiel Mphahlele says in his *African Image*—the sensitive point of his community. The Ghanaian professor of philosophy, William Abraham, put it this way:

> Just as African scientists undertake to solve some of the scientific problems of Africa, African historians go into the history of Africa, African political scientists concern themselves with the politics of Africa; why should African literary creators be exempted from the services that they themselves recognize as genuine?

I, for one, would not wish to be excused. I would be quite satisfied if my novels (especially the ones I set in the past) did no more than teach my readers that their past—with all its imperfections—was not one long night of savagery from which the first Europeans acting on God's behalf delivered them. Perhaps what I write is applied art as distinct from pure. But who cares? Art is important, but so is education of the kind I have in mind. And I don't see that the two need be mutually antagonistic. In a recent anthology, a Hausa folk tale, having recounted the usual fabulous incidents, ends with these words:

> They all came and they lived happily together. He had several sons and daughters who grew up and

helped in raising the standard of education of the country.

As I said elsewhere, if you consider this ending a naïve anticlimax, then you cannot know very much about Africa.

1965

WHERE ANGELS FEAR TO TREAD

Most Nigerian writers have at one time or another complained about European (and American) critics. The most recent example was the article by J. P. Clark in the last number of *Nigeria Magazine* entitled "Our Literary Critics." Does all this mean that Nigerian writers are intolerant of criticism as one of the assaulted critics has suggested?

I don't think so. Anyone who knows the Nigerian literary scene must be aware of the constant swiping that goes on all around. Some observers at the last Writers' Conference in Uganda commented on the way we criticized ourselves and poked fun at each other's work without rancor. No. We are not opposed to criticism, but we are getting a little weary of all the special types of criticism which have been designed for us by people whose knowledge of us is very limited. Perhaps being unused to the in-fighting which is part of the racket of European and American literary criticism, we tend to be unduly touchy and sometimes use extravagantly strong language in reply. I have been a little concerned at the

involuntary shrillness which has lately crept into my own
voice. Only the other day I wrote in an unworthy access
of anger that Europeans can never understand us and
that they ought to shut their traps. I now want to look at
the matter again as coldly as possible and try to reach a
few tentative conclusions.

The first big point to remember is that Nigerian writers
cannot eat their cake (or *eba*, or whatever they eat) and
have it. They cannot borrow a world language to write
in, seek publication in Europe and America, and then
expect the world not to say something about their product,
even if that were desirable. No, we have brought home
ant-ridden faggots and must be ready for the visit of
lizards. In part we should see it as a great compliment
that in the ten years since we first broke into the world
with *Palm-Wine Drinkard* we are already engaging seriously the attention of critics.

The question then is not whether we should be criticized or not, but what kind of criticism. We as writers
cannot, of course, choose the kind of criticism we shall
get. But surely we can say why we hate a lot of what we
get.

I can distinguish three broad types of critics. First,
the peevishly hostile, what-do-they-think-they-are, Honor
Tracy breed. These are angry with the newfangled ideas
of colonial freedom and its gross ingratitude for colonial
benefits, and they take it out on our literature. They won't
be missed.

Then there are others who are amazed that we should
be able to write at all, and in their own language too! I
must admit they have their hearts in the right place—
rather like the German traveler who published a book,
Through African Doors, recently. This man made a num-

ber of discoveries, one of which was that African food was not really monotonous as some people thought, although it must be admitted that its color rarely deviates from red, green, and yellow. Was it any wonder, he asked, that the flags of Ghana, Guinea, and Cameroun were red, green, and yellow!

This type (whether he is a critic or a writer) won't be missed very much.

Fortunately there is a third group which is fully conscious of the folly of the other two and is bent on restoring a sense of balance to the argument. This third group says: We must apply to these African writers the same stringent standards of literary criticism with which we judge other writers. We don't have to pat them on the back and make them think they have already written masterpieces when we know they haven't.

This is a group with whom we could hold a dialogue, with frankness on either side. So let us begin.

This group annoys us by their increasing dogmatism. The other day one of them spoke of the great African novel yet to be written. He said the trouble with what we have written so far is that it has concentrated too much on society and not sufficiently on individual characters and as a result it has lacked "true" aesthetic proportions. I wondered when this *truth* became so self-evident and who decided that (unlike the other self-evident truth) this one should apply to black as well as white.

It is all this cocksureness which I find so very annoying.

Another European critic was writing recently about Cyprian Ekwensi's *Burning Grass*. It was clear that this critic preferred it to the author's earlier books, *People of the City* and *Jagua Nana*. So far so good. But the critic went further to make pronouncements she was not qualified to make. She said of *Burning Grass:* "This is truly Nigerian and these are *real* Nigerian people." She did not say what her test was for sorting out real Nigerians from unreal ones and what makes, say, Jagua less real than Sunsaye. And as if that was not enough, this critic went on to say that Ekwensi was much more at home in a rural setting than in big cities!

This kind of judgment is made all too frequently by Europeans who think they have special knowledge of Africa.

Let us examine for a brief moment the quality of this special knowledge.

I had a European friend, Mr. X, who was very fond of his steward whom we shall call Cletus. Mr. X found Cletus terribly amusing because his inadequate knowledge of English made him say things in a fresh and funny way just as a child does when it is learning to talk. Mr. X spoke of Cletus' infantile qualities with affectionate indulgence. "He is a rogue," said Mr. X, "but a nice sort of rogue."

I used to speak to Cletus in Ibo and I knew that he was a shrewd go-getter, neither shallow nor very amusing.

If Mr. X had been a novelist he might have written about Cletus the harmless, "I-like-Master-too-much" steward; and other Europeans would have said "How true! Real Nigeria!"

I am not saying that the picture of Nigeria and Nigerians painted by a conscientious European must be invalid. I think it could be terribly valid, just as a picture of the visible tenth of an iceberg is valid.

I am sure that European writers on Africa are conscious of this kind of validity hence their efforts to describe the other nine tenths. The result is the man-of-two-worlds bogey—something lurking down there beyond the reach of Western education, the Guinea "stamp of one defect."

But theories and bogeys are no substitute for insight. No man can understand another whose language he does not speak (and "language" here does not mean simply words, but a man's entire world-view). How many Europeans and Americans know our language? I do not know of any, certainly not among our writers and critics.

This naturally applies also in reverse, although our position is somewhat stronger because we have a good deal of European history, philosophy, culture, etc., in books. Even so, I would not dream of constructing theories to explain "the European mind" with the same "bold face" that some Europeans assume in explaining ours. But perhaps I am too diffident and ought to have a go at it. After all a novel is only a story and could be as tall as an iroko tree; in any case one couldn't do worse than the author of *Bribe Scorner's* who invented an Ibo hero with a Yoruba name.

1962

THOUGHTS ON THE AFRICAN NOVEL

When I was first invited to this conference,[1] I was asked to speak about the African writer and the English language. I fired back a flat *No!* Then I was asked to say what I should prefer to talk about. I said nothing; I had no idea what I wanted to talk about. Finally I was confronted with a *fait accompli* in the form of a printed program in which "The African Novel" was put down against my name. I had then to accept, having twice already proved unco-operative and ungracious.

But as it happened, I had just about this time resolved not to make any further pronouncements on the African novel or African literature or any of these large topics unless I dreamt up something really novel and spectacular to say. But perhaps the day-to-day thoughts and worries are just as important, being always with us. So I give them to you.

Many years ago, at a writers' conference in Makerere,

[1] A conference on African literature at Dalhousie University, Halifax, Canada, May 1973.

Uganda, I attempted (not very successfully) to get my colleagues to defer a definition of African literature which was causing us a lot of trouble. I suggested that the task might become easier when more of our produce had entered the market. That was ten years ago. I was saying in effect that African literature would define itself in action; so why not leave it alone? I still think it was excellent advice even if it carried a hint of evasiveness or even superstition.

I do admit to certain residual superstitions; and one of the strongest is the fear of names, of hurrying to a conclusion when the issue is still wide open. If I may paraphrase a proverb which seems to me appropriate: *Do not underrate a day while an hour of light remains.* In other words, be careful, for one hour is enough to do a man in.

Edogo's mind was in pain over the child. Some people were already saying that perhaps he was none other than the first one. But Edogo and Amoge never talked about it; the woman especially was afraid. Since utterance had power to change fear into living truth, they dared not speak before they had to.

The world of the creative artist is like that. It is not the world of the taxonomist whose first impulse on seeing a new plant or animal is to define, classify, and file away. Nor is it the world of the taxidermist who plies an even less desirable trade.

But I am never fully consistent, not even in my superstitions. I always find thoughts antagonistic to my secure position floating dangerously around it. It is these floating thoughts I wish to talk to you about.

The first is that the African novel has to be about Africa. A pretty severe restriction, I am told. But Africa is not only a geographical expression, it is also a metaphysical landscape—it is, in fact, a view of the world and of the whole cosmos perceived from a particular position. This is as close to the brink of chaos as I dare proceed. As for who an African novelist is, it is partly a matter of passports, of individual volition, and particularly of seeing from that perspective I have just touched with the timidity of a snail's horn. Being an African, like being a Jew, carries certain penalties—as well as benefits, of course. But perhaps more penalties than benefits. Ben Gurion once said: *If somebody wants to be a Jew, that's enough for me.* We could say the same for being an African. So it is futile to argue whether Conrad's *Heart of Darkness* is African literature. As far as I know, Joseph Conrad never even considered the possibility. In spite of all temptations, he remained an Englishman! And it is not even a matter of color. For we have Nadine Gordimer (who is here today), Doris Lessing, and others.

And then language. As you know there has been an impassioned controversy about an African literature in non-African languages. But what is a *non-African* language? English and French certainly. But what about Arabic? What about Swahili even? Is it then a question of how long the language has been present on African soil? If so, how many years should constitute *effective occupation?* For me it is again a pragmatic matter. A language spoken by Africans on African soil, a language in which Africans write, justifies itself.

I fully realize that I am beginning to sound like a bad dictionary—the type you take a strange word to and it defines it with a stranger word; you look *that* up and it gives you back your original strange word; so you end up with two mysteries instead of one! But that is the reality of our situation, and it is surely more useful to begin to deal with its complexity than propose catchy but impossible simplifications.

At the root of all these strange and untidy thoughts lies a monumental historical fact, Europe—a presence which has obsessed us from Equiano to Ekwensi. For Equiano, a preoccupation with Europe was pretty inevitable. After all, he had only just recently freed himself from actual enslavement to Europeans. He lived in Europe and was married to a European. His ancestral Igboland had become a fragmented memory.

In our own time a preoccupation with Europe has seemed almost equally inevitable despite the passage of nearly two hundred years. In the colonial period and its aftermath, we were preoccupied with Europe in the form of protest. Then a bunch of bright ones came along and said: "We are through with intoning the colonial litany. We hereby repudiate the crippling legacy of a Europe-oriented protest. We are tough-minded. We absolve Europe of all guilt. Don't you worry, Europe, we were bound to violence long before you came to our shores." Naturally Europe, which was beginning to believe the worst about itself, is greatly relieved and impressed by the mental emancipation, objectivity, and sophistication of these newcomers. As if any intelligent writer of protest had ever taken a starry-eyed view of Africa, or doubted the reality of evil in Africa, the new antiprotest, broad-minded writer will now endorse the racist theory that Africa *is* evil, *is* the heart of darkness.

It is this illusion of objectivity, this grotesque considerateness, this perverse charitableness which asks a man to cut his own throat for the comfort and good opinion of another that I must now address myself to.

Quite often the malady (for it is indeed a sickness) shows fairly mild symptoms and is widespread; at other times it comes in its virulent forms. But mild or severe, it manifests itself as self-disgust and an obscene eagerness to please our adversary.

There is a Nigerian academic who went to study in Britain in the late 1920s and decided to become an Englishman. So he settled down in Britain after his studies, married, and raised a family and, by all accounts, was a perfectly happy man. Forty years later, as a result of an unhappy conjunction of events, he found himself appointed to an administrative position in a Nigerian university. To his first press interviewer he boasted that he spoke no Nigerian language. He cannot recognize Nigerian food, let alone eat it. Given a chance he will appoint a European over a Nigerian to teach at his university; his argument: a university, as the name implies, is a universal institution.

But, fortunately, this man is not a writer. For wouldn't it be awful if writers—those bright hopes of our society—should become afflicted with such a warped vision; a vision which creates a false polarity between an object and its abstraction and places its focus on the abstraction? Personally I am no longer entirely optimistic. Let me present two short passages of the kind that has been causing me great discomfort:

This is the confrontation which *The Interpreters* presents. It is not an "African" problem. Events all over the world have shown in the new generation a similar dissatisfaction. . . . Thus Soyinka, using a

Nigerian setting, has portrayed a universal problem. This is what makes both this novel and the whole corpus of Soyinka's work universally valid.

(Eldred Jones—*The Essential Soyinka*)

Before I go on, let me make two points. First, I am not in disagreement with Professor Eldred Jones's evaluation of Soyinka but with the terms he has chosen for that evaluation. The second point is that I regard Eldred Jones as our finest literary scholar, a man of great sensitivity and perception whom I should have much preferred not to disagree with. But the dogma of universality which he presents here (I believe, absent-mindedly) is so patently false and dangerous, and yet so attractive, that it ought not to go unchallenged. For supposing "events all over the world" have *not* shown "in the new generation a similar dissatisfaction . . ." would it truly be invalid for a Nigerian writer seeing a dissatisfaction in *his* society to write about it? Am I being told for Christ's sake that before I write about any problem I must first verify whether they have it too in New York and London and Paris?

What Professor Eldred Jones is proposing is that I renounce my vision which (since I do not work with the radio telescope at Joddrel Bank) is necessarily local and particular. Not so long ago a similar proposition was made to me, an attempt to discredit my vision and the absolute validity of my experience. But it came from "expected quarters." At the end of the war in Nigeria (in which, you may know, I was on the wrong side), I had an invitation to visit New Guinea and Australia. But some official, or officials, in Lagos saw to it that I did not get a passport. When I protested to the Commissioner for External Affairs, he wrote me a nice, intriguing letter with words to this effect:

Dear Achebe,

Thank you for your letter in which you complained about difficulties which you thought you had with my officials. . . .

You can see, can't you, the close kinship between that letter and the proposition by Eldred Jones? They are both telling me to be careful in defining "difficulties." Because other people may not agree, I had better check my vision with them before saying what I see. Such a proposition is dangerous and totally unacceptable, for once you agree to "clear" your vision with other people, you are truly in trouble. Now let us look at another short extract from the same essay by Eldred Jones in a book called *Introduction to Nigerian Literature*:

When Wole Soyinka writes like this his audience is not a local one; it is a universal one. Indeed at this point he widens his immediate range of reference by making the Court Historian invoke the precedent of the Trojan War.

Thus in the first extract Eldred Jones praises Wole Soyinka for not writing about an African problem but a universal one; and in the second for not writing for a local but a universal audience! Surely, African criticism must be the only one in the whole world (or perhaps universe) where literary merit is predicated on such outlandish criteria. But as I said earlier I don't really believe that

Eldred Jones thought seriously about this. He has simply and uncritically accepted the norms of some of the prevailing colonialist criticism, which I must say is most unlike him. Perhaps I should point out in fairness, also, that in the first extract he did put *African* in quotes, although it is not clear to me what exactly the quotes are supposed to do. Perhaps they hint at a distinction between *real* and *so-called* African problems. This may redeem the situation somewhat, but not very much. For *real* and *so-called* Africa can and do become metaphysical retreats for all kinds of prejudice. Thus a certain critic many years ago said of Ekwensi's *Burning Grass:* "At last Ekwensi has drawn real Nigerian characters . . ." without saying what unreal Nigerian characters looked like. But one sensed that a Lagosian or an African from Nairobi might be deemed less real than a Masai or a Tuareg, surely a matter of social taste and not of literary criticism!

I shall look at one other aspect of the same problem and I shall be done. In our discussion yesterday, Professor Emile Snyder reminded us that politics was always present in literature and gave examples ranging from Dante to Eliot. Why, he asked, do we get so worked up about it in discussing African literature? Of course the reason is that we are late starters. I mean really late—after the prizes are all given out and the track judges have packed up their things and gone home. Such late starters are generally very conscientious. Though no one is looking, they will cut no corners.

That is why, for instance, we must now have our own debate on art for art's sake; why we must have pundits decreeing to us what is or is not appropriate to literature; what genres are for us and what we may only touch at our peril; why literary legislators pass laws telling us what social and political roles artists may (but more usually, may not) perform.

Thus in a curious novel entitled *The Trial of Christopher Okigbo,* Ali Mazrui has a poet tried in the hereafter for throwing away his life on the battlefield like any common tribesman. There is no condemnation of war as such, only of poets getting involved—for "some lives are more sacred than others." In the words of one of the novel's leading characters (an African Perry Mason clearly admired by Mazrui):

> a great artist was first of all an individualist, secondly a universalist, and only thirdly a social collectivist.

Since these roles and attributes are not known instinctively by the artist in question (otherwise how would Okigbo not know what was legitimate activity for him?), it stands to reason that he requires some one like Mazrui to tell him (a) the precise moment when he crosses the threshold of mere artist and becomes a great artist and (b) how to juggle with his three marbles of individualism, universalism, and social collectivism.

What I am saying really boils down to a simple plea for the African novel. Don't fence me in.

I dare not close without a word of recognition for that small and proprietary school of critics, which assures us that the African novel does not exist. Reason: the novel was invented in England. For the same kind of reason, I shouldn't know how to drive a car because I am no descendant of Henry Ford. But every visitor to Nigeria will tell you that we are among the world's most creative drivers!

Only fifteen years ago a bright, skeptical academic at

a Nigerian university could raise a laugh by saying: *That would be the day when English literature is taught from Chaucer to Achebe.* Today, I much regret to say, that same academic makes a living teaching African literature in some cozy corner of the globe, presumably teaching more Achebe than Chaucer. Na so ˌdis worl' be.

In conclusion, all these prescriptions and proscriptions, all these dogmas about the universal and the eternal verities, all this proselytizing for European literary fashions, even dead ones, all this hankering after definitions may in the end prove worse than futile by creating needless anxieties. For as everybody knows anxiety can hinder creative performance, from sex to science.

I have no doubt at all about the existence of the African novel. This form of fiction has seized the imagination of many African writers and they will use it according to their differing abilities, sensibilities, and visions without seeking any one's permission. I believe it will grow and prosper. I believe it has a great future.

Recently one of my students pointed to a phrase on the cover of Camara Laye's *The Radiance of the King* and said "Do you agree with that?" It was a comment credited to my good friend, Ezekiel Mphahlele, to the effect that this was "the great African novel." I told the student that I had nothing to say because I had an interest in the matter: and I'm glad to say, the joke was well taken. Actually, I admire *The Radiance of the King* quite a lot; still I do hope that the great African novel will not be about a disreputable European.

1973

THE AFRICAN WRITER AND THE ENGLISH LANGUAGE

In June 1952, there was a writers' gathering at Makerere, impressively styled: "A Conference of African Writers of English Expression." Despite this sonorous and rather solemn title, it turned out to be a very lively affair and a very exciting and useful experience for many of us. But there was something which we tried to do and failed—that was to define "African literature" satisfactorily.

Was it literature produced *in* Africa or *about* Africa? Could African literature be on any subject, or must it have an African theme? Should it embrace the whole continent or south of the Sahara, or just *Black* Africa? And then the question of language. Should it be in indigenous African languages or should it include Arabic, English, French, Portuguese, Afrikaans, et cetera?

In the end we gave up trying to find an answer, partly —I should admit—on my own instigation. Perhaps we should not have given up so easily. It seems to me from some of the things I have since heard and read that we may have given the impression of not knowing what we were doing, or worse, not daring to look too closely at it.

A Nigerian critic, Obi Wali, writing in *Transition 10* said: "Perhaps the most important achievement of the conference . . . is that African literature as now defined and understood leads nowhere."

I am sure that Obi Wali must have felt triumphantly vindicated when he saw the report of a different kind of conference held later at Fourah Bay to discuss African literature and the University curriculum. This conference produced a tentative definition of African literature as follows: "Creative writing in which an African setting is authentically handled or to which experiences originating in Africa are integral." We are told specifically that Conrad's *Heart of Darkness* qualifies as African literature while Graham Greene's *Heart of the Matter* fails because it could have been set anywhere outside Africa.

A number of interesting speculations issue from this definition which admittedly is only an interim formulation designed to produce an indisputably desirable end, namely, to introduce African students to literature set in their environment. But I could not help being amused by the curious circumstance in which Conrad, a Pole, writing in English could produce African literature while Peter Abrahams would be ineligible should he write a novel based on his experiences in the West Indies.

What all this suggests to me is that you cannot cram African literature into a small, neat definition. I do not see African literature as one unit but as a group of associated units—in fact the sum total of all the *national* and *ethnic* literatures of Africa.

A national literature is one that takes the whole nation

for its province and has a realized or potential audience throughout its territory. In other words a literature that is written in the *national* language. An ethnic literature is one which is available only to one ethnic group within the nation. If you take Nigeria as an example, the national literature, as I see it, is the literature written in English; and the ethnic literatures are in Hausa, Ibo, Yoruba, Efik, Edo, Ijaw, etc., etc.

Any attempt to define African literature in terms which overlook the complexities of the African scene at the material time is doomed to failure. After the elimination of white rule shall have been completed, the single most important fact in Africa in the second half of the twentieth century will appear to be the rise of individual nation-states. I believe that African literature will follow the same pattern.

What we tend to do today is to think of African literature as a newborn infant. But in fact what we have is a whole generation of newborn infants. Of course, if you only look cursorily, one infant is pretty much like another; but in reality each is already set on its own separate journey. Of course, you may group them together on the basis of anything you choose—the color of their hair, for instance. Or you may group them together on the basis of the language they will speak or the religion of their fathers. Those would all be valid distinctions; but they could not begin to account fully for each individual person carrying, as it were, his own little, unique lodestar of genes.

Those who in talking about African literature want to exclude North Africa because it belongs to a different tradition surely do not suggest that Black Africa is anything like homogeneous. What does Shabaan Robert have in common with Christopher Okigbo or Awoonor-Williams? Or Mongo Beti of Cameroun and Paris with Nzekwu of Nigeria? What does the champagne-drinking upper-class Creole society described by Easmon of Sierra Leone have in common with the rural folk and fishermen of J. P. Clark's plays? Of course, some of these differences could be accounted for on individual rather than national grounds, but a good deal of it is also environmental.

I have indicated somewhat offhandedly that the national literature of Nigeria and of many other countries of Africa is, or will be, written in English. This may sound like a controversial statement, but it isn't. All I have done has been to look at the reality of present-day Africa. This "reality" may change as a result of deliberate, e.g., political, action. If it does, an entirely new situation will arise, and there will be plenty of time to examine it. At present it may be more profitable to look at the scene as it is.

What are the factors which have conspired to place English in the position of national language in many parts of Africa? Quite simply the reason is that these nations were created in the first place by the intervention of the British which, I hasten to add, is not saying that the peoples comprising these nations were invented by the British.

The country which we know as Nigeria today began not so very long ago as the arbitrary creation of the British. It is true, as William Fagg says in his excellent new book, *Nigerian Images*, that this arbitrary action has proved as lucky in terms of African art history as any enterprise of the fortunate Princess of Serendip. And I believe that in political and economic terms too this arbitrary creation called Nigeria holds out great prospects. Yet the fact remains that Nigeria was created by the British—for their own ends. Let us give the devil his due: colonialism in Africa disrupted many things, but it did create big political units where there were small, scattered ones before. Nigeria had hundreds of autonomous communities ranging in size from the vast Fulani Empire founded by Usman dan Fodio in the north to tiny village entities in the east. Today it is one country.

Of course there are areas of Africa where colonialism divided up a single ethnic group among two or even three powers. But on the whole it did bring together many peoples that had hitherto gone their several ways. And it gave them a language with which to talk to one another. If it failed to give them a song, it at least gave them a tongue, for sighing. There are not many countries in Africa today where you could abolish the language of the erstwhile colonial powers and still retain the facility for mutual communication. Therefore those African writers who have chosen to write in English or French are not unpatriotic smart alecks with an eye on the main chance —outside their own countries. They are by-products of the same process that made the new nation-states of Africa.

You can take this argument a stage further to include other countries of Africa. The only reason why we can even talk about African unity is that when we get together we can have a manageable number of languages to talk in—English, French, Arabic.

The other day I had a visit from Joseph Kariuki of Kenya. Although I had read some of his poems and he had read my novels, we had not met before. But it didn't seem to matter. In fact I had met him through his poems, especially through his love poem, *Come Away My Love,* in which he captures in so few words the trials and tensions of an African in love with a white girl in Britain:

> Come away, my love, from streets
> Where unkind eyes divide
> And shop windows reflect our difference.

By contrast, when in 1960 I was traveling in East Africa and went to the home of the late Shabaan Robert, the Swahili poet of Tanganyika, things had been different. We spent some time talking about writing, but there was no real contact. I knew from all accounts that I was talking to an important writer, but of the nature of his work I had no idea. He gave me two books of his poems which I treasure but cannot read—until I have learned Swahili.

And there are scores of languages I would want to learn if it were possible. Where am I to find the time to learn the half dozen or so Nigerian languages, each of which can sustain a literature? I am afraid it cannot be done. These languages will just have to develop as tributaries to feed the one central language enjoying nationwide currency. Today, for good or ill, that language is English. Tomorrow it may be something else, although I very much doubt it.

Those of us who have inherited the English language may not be in a position to appreciate the value of the inheritance. Or we may go on resenting it because it came as part of a package deal which included many other items of doubtful value and the positive atrocity of racial arrogance and prejudice which may yet set the world on fire. But let us not in rejecting the evil throw out the good with it.

Some time last year I was traveling in Brazil meeting

Brazilian writers and artists. A number of the writers I spoke to were concerned about the restrictions imposed on them by their use of the Portuguese language. I remember a woman poet saying she had given serious thought to writing in French! And yet their problem is not half as difficult as ours. Portuguese may not have the universal currency of English or French but at least it is the national language of Brazil with her eighty million or so people, to say nothing of the people of Portugal, Angola, Mozambique, etc.

Of Brazilian authors I have only read, in translation, one novel by Jorge Amado, who is not only Brazil's leading novelist but one of the most important writers in the world. From that one novel, *Gabriella*, I was able to glimpse something of the exciting Afro-Latin culture which is the pride of Brazil and is quite unlike any other culture. Jorge Amado is only one of the many writers Brazil has produced. At their national writers' festival there were literally hundreds of them. But the work of the vast majority will be closed to the rest of the world forever, including no doubt the work of some excellent writers. There is certainly a great advantage to writing in a world language.

I think I have said enough to give an indication of my thinking on the importance of the world language which history has forced down our throats. Now let us look at some of the most serious handicaps. And let me say straightaway that one of the most serious handicaps is *not* the one people talk about most often, namely, that it is impossible for anyone ever to use a second language as effectively as his first. This assertion is compounded of half truth and half bogus mystique. Of course, it is true that the vast majority of people are happier with their

first language than with any other. But then the majority
of people are not writers. We do have enough examples
of writers who have performed the feat of writing effectively in a second language. And I am not thinking of the
obvious names like Conrad. It would be more germane to
our subject to choose African examples.

The first name that comes to my mind is Olauda
Equiano, better known as Gustavus Vassa, the African.
Equiano was an Ibo, I believe from the village of Iseke
in the Orlu division of Eastern Nigeria. He was sold as a
slave at a very early age and transported to America.
Later he bought his freedom and lived in England. In
1789 he published his life story, a beautifully written doc-
ument which, among other things, set down for the Europe of his time something of the life and habit of his
people in Africa, in an attempt to counteract the lies and
slander invented by some Europeans to justify the slave
trade.

Coming nearer to our times, we may recall the attempts
in the first quarter of this century by West African nationalists to come together and press for a greater say in
the management of their own affairs. One of the most
eloquent of that band was the Honorable Casely Hayford
of the Gold Coast. His presidential address to the National Congress of British West Africa in 1925 was memorable not only for its sound common sense but as a fine
example of elegant prose. The governor of Nigeria at the
time was compelled to take notice and he did so in
characteristic style: he called Hayford's Congress "a self-
selected and self-appointed congregation of educated
African gentlemen." We may derive some amusement
from the fact that British colonial administrators learned
very little in the following quarter of a century. But at

least they *did* learn in the end—which is more than one can say for some others.

It is when we come to what is commonly called creative literature that most doubt seems to arise. Obi Wali, whose article "Dead End of African Literature" I referred to, has this to say:

". . . until these writers and their Western midwives accept the fact that any true African literature must be written in African languages, they would be merely pursuing a dead end, which can only lead to sterility, uncreativity and frustration."

But far from leading to sterility, the work of many new African writers is full of the most exciting possibilities. Take this from Christopher Okigbo's *Limits:*

> Suddenly becoming talkative
>   like weaverbird
> Summoned at offside of
>   dream remembered
> Between sleep and waking
> I hand up my egg-shells
> To you of palm grove,
> Upon whose bamboo towers hang
> Dripping with yesterupwine
> A tiger mask and nude spear. . . .
>
> Queen of the damp half light,
>   I have had my cleansing.
> Emigrant with air-borne nose,
>   The he-goat-on-heat.

Or take the poem, *Night Rain,* in which J. P. Clark captures so well the fear and wonder felt by a child as rain clamors on the thatch roof at night and his mother, walking about in the dark, moves her simple belongings

> Out of the run of water
> That like ants filing out of the wood
> Will scatter and gain possession
> Of the floor. . . .

I think that the picture of water spreading on the floor "like ants filing out of the wood" is beautiful. Of course if you had never made fire with faggots, you may miss it. But Clark's inspiration derives from the same source which gave birth to the saying that a man who brings home ant-ridden faggots must be ready for the visit of lizards.

I do not see any signs of sterility anywhere here. What I do see is a new voice coming out of Africa, speaking of African experience in a world-wide language. So my answer to the question *Can an African ever learn English well enough to be able to use it effectively in creative writing?* is certainly yes. If on the other hand you ask: *Can he ever learn to use it like a native speaker?* I should say, I hope not. It is neither necessary nor desirable for him to be able to do so. The price a world language must be prepared to pay is submission to many different kinds of use. The African writer should aim to use English in a way that brings out his message best without altering the language to the extent that its value as a medium of international exchange will be lost. He should aim at fashioning out an English which is at once universal and able to carry his peculiar experience. I have in mind here the writer who has something new, something different to say. The nondescript writer has little to tell us, anyway, so he might as well tell it in conventional language and get it over with. If I may use an extravagant simile, he is like a man offering a small, nondescript routine sacrifice for which a chick, or less, will do. A serious writer must look for an animal whose blood can match the power of his offering.

In this respect Amos Tutola is a natural. A good instinct has turned his apparent limitation in language into a weapon of great strength—a half-strange dialect that serves him perfectly in the evocation of his bizarre world. His last book, and to my mind, his finest, is proof enough that one can make even an imperfectly learned second language do amazing things. In this book, *The Feather Woman of the Jungle*, Tutola's superb storytelling is at last cast in the episodic form which he handles best instead of being painfully stretched on the rack of the novel.

From a natural to a conscious artist: myself, in fact. Allow me to quote a small example from *Arrow of God*, which may give some idea of how I approach the use of English. The Chief Priest in the story is telling one of his sons why it is necessary to send him to church:

> I want one of my sons to join these people and be my eyes there. If there is nothing in it you will come back. But if there is something there you will bring home my share. The world is like a Mask, dancing. If you want to see it well you do not stand in one place. My spirit tells me that those who do not befriend the white man today will be saying *had we known* tomorrow.

Now supposing I had put it another way. Like this for instance:

I am sending you as my representative among these people—just to be on the safe side in case the new religion develops. One has to move with the times or else one is left behind. I have a hunch that those who fail to come to terms with the white man may well regret their lack of foresight.

The material is the same. But the form of the one is *in character* and the other is not. It is largely a matter of instinct, but judgment comes into it too.

You read quite often nowadays of the problems of the African writer having first to think in his mother tongue and then to translate what he has thought into English. If it were such a simple, mechanical process, I would agree that it was pointless—the kind of eccentric pursuit you might expect to see in a modern Academy of Lagado; and such a process could not possibly produce some of the exciting poetry and prose which is already appearing.

One final point remains for me to make. The real question is not whether Africans *could* write in English but whether they *ought to*. Is it right that a man should abandon his mother tongue for someone else's? It looks like a dreadful betrayal and produces a guilty feeling.

But for me there is no other choice. I have been given this language and I intend to use it. I hope, though, that there always will be men, like the late Chief Fagunwa, who will choose to write in their native tongue and insure that our ethnic literature will flourish side by side with the national ones. For those of us who opt for English, there is much work ahead and much excitement.

Writing in the London *Observer* recently, James Baldwin said:

> My quarrel with the English language has been that the language reflected none of my experience. But now I began to see the matter another way. . . . Perhaps the language was not my own because I had never attempted to use it, had only learned to imitate it. If this were so, then it might be made to bear the burden of my experience if I could find the stamina to challenge it, and me, to such a test.

I recognize, of course, that Baldwin's problem is not exactly mine, but I feel that the English language will be able to carry the weight of my African experience. But it will have to be a new English, still in full communion with its ancestral home but altered to suit its new African surroundings.

1964

PUBLISHING IN AFRICA:
A Writer's View

A small co-operative press just created, owned and managed by a handful of new poets in Cambridge, Massachusetts, has described a traditional publisher in these words.

> . . . another corporation of merchandisers aimed at pushing books, like dead objects, from the warehouse to the remainder bins by the fastest possible route.

> (Alice James Books announcement)

We all know some publishers who are rather better than that! But there is a good reason for the shrillness in the voice of those unpublished New England poets. It is a tendency when we speak of books to forget or to give inadequate thought to the simple fact that our central purpose is a dialogue, or the desire for a dialogue, between writers and their readers, that everybody else in the business is a facilitator. When we speak of the *book trade* we blur the difference between merchandising and a very delicate process of bringing one human mind into communion with the minds of his fellows. This process is not akin to the cloth trade or the beer trade. When I put on a shirt, I am not in communion with the factory hand who made the yarn nor even with the tailor who sewed it (especially if it is mass produced). When I drink, I do not think of the man in the brewery who saw the bottle fill with lager or pressed the button that sealed the cap. But when I read, somebody is talking to me; and when I write, I am talking to somebody. It is a personal, intimate relationship.

The fact that this intimate purpose can best be achieved with the help of certain intermediaries does not make the mediation bigger than the primary purpose.

Apart from publishers there are other intermediaries between the writer and his readers. There are booksellers and librarians, and there are critics. (I am leaving printers out because, in practical terms today, they are technical arms of publishing and are rarely in direct contact with either writer or reader.)

These intermediaries are, of course, extremely important. None of them is, or should be, a mindless conduit or a conveyor belt "pushing books like dead objects." They do have and exercise preferences and taste. They are discriminating. A publisher does not publish everything that comes his way; a bookseller or a librarian does not stock every title published. And as for critics, have not their exploits and idiosyncracies become legendary?

In an ideal and healthy literary environment, the powers which these intermediaries exercise should work to the ultimate good of writers and their readers. For example, the publisher should winnow out a good deal of chaff so that the reader, hard pressed for time and money, may invest what he does have fruitfully and to the best advantage.

The bookseller and the librarian introduce further refinements into the system. They select from the publisher's total offering those items which their specialized knowledge tells them are of particular value and interest to the community they are out to serve.

And finally the critic by judicious bestowal of praise, and administration of rebuke on specific offerings, helps to sharpen the reader's ability to appraise and to choose. Our primary concern this week[1] must center on publishers because that is what we have been invited to talk about but also, I think, because a publisher is really more crucial than the other intermediaries. For the bookseller can only sell what the publisher issues and a critic evaluates only books that are published (or so we hope). But the crucial decision, whether this particular book is to be or not to be, belongs to the publisher.

Thus the publisher is the primary go-between from writer to reader in what I see as a dynamic social-artistic relationship. I see him even in the role of an evangelist: publishing, broadcasting the good news, traversing time and space which the original lone voice unaided could never have hoped to reach, making the inner world of the artist available to the wider world of his community by using one of man's most profoundly important technologies—printing.

I believe that a spiritual bond exists between the true artist and his community. It is not my concern if some

[1] A slightly different version of this paper was read at a conference on Publishing in Africa at the University of Ife, Nigeria, in December 1973.

people have lost that sense, and even worse, lost a sense of their loss. But we must assume that as long as writers take the trouble to write and to get themselves published, they do want to be heard and are reaching out to a community, "straining thin among the echoes" to quote Christopher Okigbo. We may argue—and may never reach total agreement—on just who comprises this community for specific writers. For the African writer, a complex situation is further confounded by mass illiteracy among his people and his use of a European language. On the face of it, he should be the loneliest of voices without any sense of community. Should be, but is he? I am more inclined to what we find than in what we think we ought to find. What do we find then when we actually read these writers? I think we find a consuming concern with community. Even those among them who have begun to make a point of their emancipated solitariness never quite come through, or come through only in fits and starts. What is this sense of community, then, this thing that breaks the laws of logic and is able to remain alive when every pointer is toward its death? I believe it is two things—the sense of a shared history and, even more important, of an assumed destiny. We are still backward enough to believe that we can go forward; old-fashioned enough to think we have a future.

When my father was a boy, there was a masked spirit in his village which was called Evil Forest. His carved headpiece was unevenly balanced, with a disproportionate part behind him, and he had a habit of asking people to say which part of this headpiece was greater: the one behind or the one in front. And in their ignorance, people would reply, basing their answer on the evidence of their eye, that what was behind was indeed greater. At which,

Evil Forest would shake his heavy head and say: *Nkiruka*
—what is in front is always greater.

I recalled this story which my father told me when I
listened to a spell-binding black American leader address-
ing an audience in New York in 1963. "Our roots are not
in the past," he said, "but in the future." Quite nonsensi-
cal, I thought at first, then I remembered Evil Forest's
words and wondered whether he and this man spoke from
a common mystical view of history which refuses to yield
to despair and which incidentally is not to be confused
with the mechanistic belief in progress, nor the improvi-
dent man's delusion that tomorrow will somehow produce its own goodies.

However, I believe that our writers derive their sense
of community from a similar unarticulated feeling of a
shared destiny, a journey toward a future. In the writer's
community, this sense may not at first rise higher than a
crude wish "to catch up" with others. Crude, but after a
year's teaching in America I must say that I am more at
home with the crude wish than the desire of others—who
have lost all faith and hope—simply to be left alone, who
like Tutuola's Simbi respond to the boredom of comfort
with a craving for punishment and poverty. If I am not
entirely deluded in my vision of the writer and his community moved together by a common destiny, of the artist and his people in a dynamic, evolving relationship,
then the go-between, the publisher, must operate in the
same historic and social continuum. It stands to reason
that he cannot play this role from London or Paris or
New York.

It may indeed be true that whatever the indigenous
publisher does, the foreign publisher can do better—for
the simple reason that the indigenous publisher does

nothing at present. Perhaps he cannot even exist in the present situation. But until he comes along, we cannot hope to have a vital literary environment.

Now I hope this will not be construed as yet another example of the native's congenital ingratitude, of his trenchant for biting off the finger that feeds him. Only the other day I saw a recent book by a British woman in which people like me were roundly admonished for not showing proper respect for the work of the District Officer which saved our mothers from oppressive male domination. So I must make it quite clear that I am indeed appreciative of the marvelous work which many foreign publishers did, and continue to do, in laying the foundation of our literature. I have personally had the best possible relationship with my British publishers and when I moved to have some of my work published initially in Nigeria they went out of their way to be co-operative.

I think it is almost certain that if we did not have foreign publishers in the 1950s, Amos Tutuola would not have seen the light of day. For him alone we should speak softly of them.

And finally we must give due recognition to the brisk move in recent years by some foreign publishers in recruiting and training Africans in various aspects of the publishing trade. Indeed, like some high-minded and wrongheaded colonialists, they have worked assiduously for their own overthrow.

But we have got to the point where our literature must grow out of the social dynamics of Africa. The role of the publisher as catalyst is no longer adequate—that of initiating and watching over a chemical reaction from a position of inviolability and emerging at the end of it all totally unchanged. What we need is an organic interaction of all three elements—writer, publisher, and reader —in a continuing state of creative energy in which all three respond to the possibilities and risks of change.

I do not wish to waste your time on a blueprint for the creation of the kind of indigenous publisher who will be capable of shouldering the responsibilities I have suggested. For one thing he would not be exactly the same sort of person in every country or region of Africa. Perhaps his greatest quality will be a liveliness of imagination which is able to seize upon the peculiar characteristics of a place and make of them a strength for his task. He would not attempt to recreate the patterns of distribution, sales, and promotion from some foreign model. He will learn what he needs to learn from others but will make his own way in the world. This does not mean he will lack method and organization. On the contrary, his bookkeeping should be so scrupulous that writers will not hesitate to place their manuscripts in his care, or booksellers to do business with him. Literary gossip travels very far and very fast, and a publisher who is a shoddy businessman will soon find no worthwhile manuscripts coming to him.

Writers, especially established writers, have a responsibility to support an indigenous publisher who displays the necessary qualities of intellect, creativity, and organization, for it is ultimately in the interests of the writer that such a publisher exists. He should be prepared to gamble on the chances of such a publisher—at least once!

It will be quite clear that the kind of pubisher I have been talking about is a private businessman. Of course he is not the only (or even the most appropriate) model conceivable. But I suppose I am under the influence of the Nigerian experience which until now has few encouraging records of state-managed industries. But even in a free-enterprise African setting, there is need for state support and patronage of indigenous publishing. For instance, with the advice of a small body of writers and educational people, the state could select three or four publishing houses on the basis of performance and help them to develop further by awards of state contracts. This selected group will have to be subjected to stringent periodic appraisal to determine whether or not they continue to merit patronage and preferential treatment.

More radically minded countries will continue to choose the state-publishing model. I suppose that ultimately the great argument against it is the elimination of all dissent. That is a strong argument, though, to my mind, not as strong as we make out when we imply that free enterprise automatically encourages the airing of dissent, surely a stupendous fallacy.

Obviously state publishing works well enough in many countries, and there is no reason why it should not work in African countries. But those who choose it should insure that it responds to the particular needs of the place, and that it should not be dominated by the record-breaking obsession which led the director of Egypt's state publishing in the early stages to boast that his enterprise published a book every six hours. In certain circumstances, it might be preferable to be less productive.

University of Ife, 1973

PART 2

NAMED FOR VICTORIA, QUEEN OF ENGLAND

I was born in Ogidi in Eastern Nigeria of devout Christian parents. The line between Christian and non-Christian was much more definite in my village forty years ago than it is today. When I was growing up I remember we tended to look down on the others. We were called in our language "the people of the church" or "the association of God." The others we called, with the conceit appropriate to followers of the true religion, the heathen or even "the people of nothing."

Thinking about it today I am not so sure that it isn't they who should have been looking down on us for our apostasy. And perhaps they did. But the bounties of the Christian God were not to be taken lightly—education, paid jobs, and many other advantages that nobody in his right senses could underrate. And in fairness we should add that there was more than naked opportunism in the defection of many to the new religion. For in some ways and in certain circumstances, it stood firmly on the side of humane behavior. It said, for instance, that twins were not evil and must no longer be abandoned in the forest to die. Think what that would have done for that unhappy woman whose heart, torn to shreds at every birth, could now hold on precariously to a new hope.

There was still considerable evangelical fervor in my early days. Once a month, in place of the afternoon church service, we went into the village with the gospel. We would sing all the way to the selected communal meeting place. Then the pastor or catechist or one of the elders, having waited for enough heathen people to assemble, would address them on the evil futility of their ways. I do not recall that we made even one conversion. On the contrary I have a distinct memory of the preacher getting into serious trouble with a villager who was apparently notorious for turning up at every occasion with a different awkward question. As you would expect this was no common villager but a fallen Christian, technically known as a *backslider*. Like Satan, a spell in heaven had armed him with unfair insights.

My father had joined the new faith as a young man and risen rapidly in its ranks to become an evangelist and church teacher. His maternal grandfather, who had brought him up (his own parents having died early), was a man of note in the village. He had taken the highest but one title that a man of wealth and honor might aspire to, and the feast he gave the town on his initiation became a byword for openhandedness bordering on prodigality. The grateful and approving community called him henceforth Udo Osinyi—Udo who cooks more than the whole people can eat.

From which you might deduce that my ancestors approved of ostentation. And you would be right. But they would probably have argued if the charge was made by their modern counterparts that in their day wealth could only be acquired honestly, by the sweat of a man's brow. They would probably never have given what I believe was the real but carefully concealed reason, namely, that given their extreme republican and egalitarian worldview, it made good sense for the community to encourage a man acquiring more wealth than his neighbors to convert that threat of material power into harmless honorific distinction, while his accumulated riches flowed back into the commonwealth.

Apparently the first missionaries who came to my village went to Udo Osinyi to pay their respects and seek support for their work. For a short while my great grandfather allowed them to operate from his compound. He probably thought it was some kind of circus whose strange presence added luster to his household. But after a few days he sent them packing again. Not, as you might think, on account of the crazy theology they had begun to propound but on the much more serious grounds of musical aesthetics. Said the old man: "Your singing is too sad to come from a man's house. My neighbors might think it was my funeral dirge."

So they parted—without rancor. When my father joined the missionaries the old man did not seem to have raised any serious objections. Perhaps like Ezeulu he thought he needed a representative in their camp. Or perhaps he thought it was a modern diversion which a young man might indulge in without coming to too much harm. He must have had second thoughts when my father began to have ideas about converting him. But it never came to an open rift; apparently not even a quarrel. They remained very close to the end. I don't know it for certain, but I think the old man was the very embodiment of tolerance, insisting only that whatever a man decided to do he should do it with style. I am told he was very pleased when my father, a teacher now, had a wedding to which white missionaries (now no longer figures of fun) came in their fineries, their men and their women, bearing gifts. He must have been impressed too by the wedding feast which might not have approached his own legendary performance but was by all accounts pretty lavish.

About ten years ago, before my father died he told me of a recent dream in which his grandfather, long, long dead, arrived at our house like a traveler from a distant land come in for a brief stop and rest and was full of admiration for the zinc house my father had built. There was something between those two that I find deep, moving, and perplexing. And of those two generations—defectors and loyalists alike—there was something I have not been able to fathom. That was why the middle story in the Okonkwo trilogy, as I originally projected it, never got written. I had suddenly become aware that in my gallery of ancestral heroes there is an empty place from which an unknown personage seems to have departed.

I was baptized Albert Chinualumogu. I dropped the tribute to Victorian England when I went to the university, although you might find some early acquaintances still calling me by it. The earliest of them all—my mother—certainly stuck to it to the bitter end. So if anyone asks you what her Britannic Majesty Queen Victoria had in common with Chinua Achebe, the answer is, They both lost their Albert! As for the second name, which in the manner of my people is a full-length philosophical statement, I simply cut it in two, making it more businesslike without, I hope, losing the general drift of its meaning.

I have always been fond of stories and intrigued by language—first Igbo, spoken with such eloquence by the old men of the village, and later English which I began to learn at about the age of eight. I don't know for certain but I have probably spoken more words in Igbo than English, but I have definitely written more words in English than Igbo. Which I think makes me perfectly bilingual. Some people have suggested that I should be better off writing in Igbo. Sometimes they seek to drive the point home by asking me in which language I dream. When I reply that I dream in both languages they seem not to believe it. More recently I have heard an even more potent and metaphysical version of the question, In what language do you have an orgasm? Which should settle the matter if I knew!

We lived at the crossroads of cultures. We still do today, but when I was a boy one could see and sense the peculiar quality and atmosphere of it more clearly. I am not talking about all that rubbish we hear of the spiritual void and mental stresses that Africans are supposed to have, or the evil forces and irrational passions prowling through Africa's heart of darkness. We know the racist mystique behind a lot of that stuff and should merely point out that those who prefer to see Africa in those lurid terms have not themselves demonstrated any clear superiority in sanity or more competence in coping with life.

But still the crossroads does have a certain dangerous potency; dangerous because a man might perish there wrestling with multiple-headed spirits, but also he might be lucky and return to his people with the boon of prophetic vision.

On one arm of the cross, we sang hymns and read the

Bible night and day. On the other, my father's brother and his family, blinded by heathenism, offered food to idols. That was how it was supposed to be anyhow. But I knew without knowing why that it was too simple a way to describe what was going on. Those idols and that food had a strange pull on me in spite of my being such a thorough little Christian that often at Sunday services at the height of the grandeur of "Te Deum laudamus" I would have dreams of a mantle of gold falling on me as the choir of angels drowned our mortal song and the voice of God Himself thundered: This is my beloved son in whom I am well pleased. Yes, despite those delusions of divine destiny I was not past taking my little sister to our neighbor's house when our parents were not looking and partaking of heathen festival meals. I never found their rice and stew to have the flavor of idolatry. I was about ten then. If anyone likes to believe that I was torn by spiritual agonies or stretched on the rack of my ambivalence, he certainly may suit himself. I do not remember any undue distress. What I do remember was a fascination for the ritual and the life on the other arm of the crossroads. And I believe two things were in my favor—that curiosity and the little distance imposed between me and it by the accident of my birth. The distance becomes not a separation but a bringing together like the necessary backward step which a judicious viewer may take in order to see a canvas steadily and fully.

I was lucky in having a few old books around the house when I was learning to read. As the fifth in a family of six children, and with parents so passionate for their children's education, I inherited many discarded primers and readers. I remember *A Midsummer Night's Dream* in an advanced stage of falling apart. I think it must have been a prose adaptation, simplified and illustrated. I don't re-

member whether I made anything of it. Except the title.
I couldn't get over the strange beauty of it. A Midsummer
Night's Dream. It was a magic phrase—an incantation
that conjured up scenes and landscapes of an alien,
happy, and unattainable land.

I remember also my mother's *Ije Onye Kraist* which
must have been an Igbo adaptation of *Pilgrim's Progress*.
It could not have been the whole book; it was too thin.
But it had some frightening pictures. I recall in particular
a most vivid impression of *the valley of the shadow of
death*. I thought a lot about death in those days. There
was another little book which frightened and fascinated
me. It had drawings of different parts of the human body.
But I was primarily interested in what my elder sister told
me was the human heart. Since there is a slight confusion
in Igbo between heart and soul, I took it that that strange
thing, looking almost like my mother's iron cooking pot
turned upside down, was the very thing that flew out when
a man died and perched on the head of the coffin on the
way to the cemetery.

I found some use for most of the books in our house but
by no means all. There was one arithmetic book I smug-
gled out and sold for half a penny which I needed to buy
the tasty *mai-mai* some temptress of a woman sold in
the little market outside the school. I was found out and
my mother who had never had cause till then to doubt
my honesty—laziness, yes; but not theft—received a huge
shock. Of course she redeemed the book. I was so
ashamed when she brought it home that I don't think I
ever looked at it again, which was probably why I never
had much use for mathematics.

My parents' reverence for books was almost superstitious, so my action must have seemed like a form of juvenile simony. My father was much worse than my

mother. He never destroyed any paper. When he died we had to make a bonfire of all the hoardings of his long life. I am the very opposite of him in this. I can't stand paper around me. Whenever I see a lot of it I am seized by a mild attack of pyromania. When I die my children will not have a bonfire.

The kind of taste I acquired from the chaotic literature in my father's house can well be imagined. For instance I became very fond of those aspects of ecclesiastical history as could be garnered from *The West African Churchman's Pamphlet*—a little terror of a booklet prescribing interminable Bible readings morning and night. It had the date of consecration for practically every Anglican bishop who ever served in West Africa, and, even more intriguing, the dates of their death. Many of them didn't last very long. I remember one pathetic case (I forget his name) who arrived in Lagos straight from his consecration at St. Paul's Cathedral and was dead within days, and his wife a week or two after him. Those were the days when West Africa was truly the white man's grave, when those great lines were written, of which I was at that time unaware:

Bight of Benin! Bight of Benin!
Where few come out though many go in!

But the most fascinating information I got from *Pamphlet*, as we called it, was this cryptic entry:

Augustine, Bishop of Hippo, died 430.

It had that elusive and eternal quality, a tantalizing unfamiliarity which I always found moving.

I did not know that I was going to be a writer because I did not really know of the existence of such creatures until fairly late. The folk stories my mother and elder sister told me had the immemorial quality of the sky and the forests and the rivers. Later, when I got to know that the European stories I read were written by known people, it still didn't help much. It was the same Europeans who made all the other marvelous things like the motor-car. We did not come into it at all. We made nothing that wasn't primitive and heathenish.

The nationalist movement in British West Africa after the Second World War brought about a mental revolution which began to reconcile us to ourselves. It suddenly seemed that we too might have a story to tell. "Rule Britannia!" to which we had marched so unselfconsciously on Empire Day now stuck in our throats.

At the university I read some appalling novels about Africa (including Joyce Cary's much praised *Mister Johnson*) and decided that the story we had to tell could not be told for us by anyone else, no matter how gifted or well-intentioned.

Although I did not set about it consciously in that solemn way I now know that my first book, *Things Fall Apart*, was an act of atonement with my past, the ritual return and homage of a prodigal son. But things happen very fast in Africa. I had hardly begun to bask in the sunshine of reconciliation when a new cloud appeared, a new estrangement. Political independence had come. The nationalist leader of yesterday (with whom it had not been too difficult to make common cause) had become the not so attractive party boss. And then things really got going. The party boss was chased out by the bright military boys, new idols of the people. But the party boss knows how to wait, knows by heart the counsel Mother Bedbug gave her little ones when the harassed owner of the bed poured hot water on them. "Be patient," said she, "for what is hot will in the end be cold." What is bright can also get tarnished, like the military boys.

One hears that the party boss is already conducting a whispering campaign. "You done see us chop," he says. "Now you see *dem* chop. Which one you like pass?" And the people are truly confused.

In a little nondescript coffee shop where I sometimes stop for a hamburger in Amherst, there are some unfunny inscriptions hanging on the walls, representing a one-sided dialogue between management and staff. The unfunniest of them all reads—poetically:

> Take care of your boss
> The next one may be worse.

The trouble with writers is that they will often refuse to live by such rationality.

1973

TANGANYIKA—*Jottings of a Tourist*

"We tell the world that we live in a happy multiracial society; it's all lies, nothing but lies. . . ." I was listening from the Visitors' Gallery to a Legislative Council debate on school integration. Date: November 1960. The African honorable member who spoke the words was promptly called to order for his unparliamentary language. But one could sense the great awkwardness engendered by an uncomfortable truth. Perhaps the much advertised difference between, say, Kenya and Tanganyika in racial tension was a difference in degree rather than kind, despite popular fiction.

Some days later, I visited the home of a rich and good-natured Asian (with children in expensive public schools in England) who complained bitterly that in spite of the large sums of money he had contributed to African charity, he was neither appreciated nor trusted. "I was born here," he said. "I have no other home."

A month later, a European club in Dar es Salaam was debating whether it ought to amend its rules so that Julius

Nyerere, Chief Minister, might be able to drink there on the invitation of a member. (It did not seem to occur to anyone that Nyerere might not wish to have the honor of drinking there.)

A European yacht club which had made its facilities available to officers of the King's African Rifles removed this concession as soon as the first African officer cadets completed their training in England. Perhaps only a coincidence.

I went to the British Council to cancel an appointment I had made (or rather, *they* had made for me) to address the local Rotary club. A European woman at the typewriter glared at me. "What do you want?" "Can I see the Representative?" "What do you want to see him for?" And so on.

A well-meaning receptionist at a second-class hotel told me as I checked in that she didn't mind Africans. She remembered with obvious pride that she once had a young African woman who behaved perfectly all the time she was in the hotel. "She spoke such *beautiful* English; I was so proud of her."

Tanganyika may well become a happy multiracial country in the future. Today it is three racial societies living in one country. And it will probably remain so as long as racial differences tend to coincide with educational, economic, and other opportunities. Multiracialism, partnership, and such other high-sounding words are meaningless unless they are applied to equals. Mr. Nyerere told the Legislative Council in October 1960 that of the 515 medical practitioners in the country only fourteen were Africans. I attended the wedding of the first and only African lawyer in the territory.

"The colonial administration simply did not train the people and we are going to train them. . . . we are going to turn out thousands of well-trained people but it is going to take us time." The words of Julius Nyerere in the Legislative Council. His government has now decided to build a university in the territory. Some experts say it is premature to build a university when there are so few secondary schools. Which reminds one that in 1944 when the Elliot Commission recommended to the British Colonial Secretary the building of *one* university for the whole of British West Africa, many experts said it was premature. Experts can often be so foolish.

A Mass Meeting of TANU

I was taken by friends to a mass meeting of the Tanganyika African National Union one hot Saturday afternoon in Dar es Salaam. There were two attractions to this particular meeting. First, one of the most popular ministers and secretary of TANU was to make his first public appearance with his bride after their highly publicized wedding at St. Paul's Cathedral in London. Secondly, it was said that the first murmurs of dissatisfaction were beginning to be heard in the party, and Nyerere was expected to deal with them.

The attraction of the newlyweds did not materialize and was soon forgotten. The vast crowd sat on the ground, while Nyerere and his party supporters took their places on a rickety-looking platform of planks and palm leaves specially built for the occasion. A number of people spoke from the platform, but the crowd sat unmoved, apparently unimpressed. It occurred to me how totally different all this was from the irrepressible ebullience of a Nigerian political crowd. For one thing a Nigerian gathering would not sit—let alone placidly.

But things soon began to warm up and look a little familiar when Madam Bibi Titi took the stage. She is the leader of the women's wing of TANU and one of Tanganyika's most formidable politicians. Stocky, middle-aged perhaps (it is difficult to guess at her age), she is a veritable terror to her enemies. Bibi Titi never went to school but taught herself English in a few months so as to meet the requirement for taking the seat she had just won in the Legislative Council. Within two minutes of Bibi Titi's getting to her feet, the placid crowd had been galvanized. The burden of her speech was an indulgent attack on Nyerere for being so lenient to his opponents. The word "democratic" stuck out frequently in her flow of Swahili speech. She mouthed it with such palpable disgust that the crowd practically rolled on the ground with laughter.

While his lieutenants spoke, Nyerere appeared completely indifferent, smoking or merely toying with his cigarette in apparent boredom. He looked frail and out of place in that robust company. I had never seen a politician appear so unconcerned about his crowd. And yet when he finally rose to his feet and began to speak he was brilliantly effective. From beginning to end the crowd never ceased to cheer and clap and laugh.

A Swahili Poet

As a West African I was amazed at the total absence of tribalism in Tanganyika. In this respect the territory is unique in Black Africa. It may be that Tanganyikan tribes were too fragmentary and small to be effective and that

Swahili was able to spread easily throughout the land. Certainly the use of this common language has made it easy for the first properly organized nationalist party to reach every corner of the country and entrench itself.

The spread of Swahili in the last hundred years has been phenomenal. A European scholar told me it was more momentous than the rise of nationalism in Africa. An unbalanced assessment, I thought, showing a forgivable partiality for a subject very dear to his heart. But the importance and potentiality of Swahili are indeed enormous. That is why every foreign power, great or small, engaged in the new scramble for Africa is daily pouring out radio programs in that language. What effect does it all have? I just wonder.

I was discussing literature with a group of young intellectuals in Nairobi before I went to Tanganyika, and one or two of them admitted quite frankly that they would not care to read a work written in Swahili. Later on in Tanga I had the privilege and rare pleasure of meeting Sheikh Shaaban Robert, the leading Swahili poet, and he was greatly depressed by the apathy of his people to Swahili literature. He told me of the difficulty he had publishing new works and how a South African university published one of his books and paid him nothing until he wrote them a letter of protest whereupon they sent him forty pounds.

With very little capital Sheikh Robert has now set up as a publisher and has brought out two books of poetry; one of them, *Masomo Yenye Adili,* I understand, is particularly good. Robert plans ultimately to publish not only his own works but those of other African writers as well.

The People of Kilimanjaro

Mount Kibo, the highest peak in the Kilimanjaro range, is at first somewhat disappointing. It simply does not look high enough to be the highest mountain in Africa. It lacks the spiritual majesty of Mount Kenya. But it grows on one. There is something of a ritual at sunset when it reveals itself from the thick mantle of cloud which hides it in the day. As night falls the white dome is lit up by the last rays of light while the foothills and the rest of the world sink into darkness. At that hour, if at none other, Mount Kibo is truly magnificent.

"The natives are not represented at this conference . . . nevertheless the decision of this body will be of the greatest importance to them." Thus spoke the British representative at the 1885 Berlin Conference. It was an unusual and quite unexpected concern for the opinion of the natives and may have been prompted not so much by democratic considerations as by the fact that Britain was unenthusiastic about the meeting itself called on Bismarck's initiative. Certainly in 1886 when Queen Victoria, with winning effrontery, presented the Kilimanjaro Mountain as a birthday present to her cousin the Kaiser, nobody thought to consult the natives.

The Wachagga are a very progressive people who inhabit the slopes of the Kilimanjaro. They are comparatively wealthy because they grow coffee on modern co-operative lines. I am told that the Wachagga used not to be very popular with the British administration, especially with one particular governor who had strong views on natives in lounge suits! The Masai took one look at Western civilization and turned their backs on it; the

Wachagga took a plunge without looking. They are always trying out new things. In the fifties they decided to unite their 300,000 people under a paramount chief and chose as their first ruler Tom Marealle, a graduate of the London School of Economics. In 1960 they declared him too ambitious and replaced him with an elected president, Solomon Eliufoo, who had studied at Makerere and the United States and was one of Mr. Nyerere's brightest ministers.

In a speech to the Chagga Council, Mr. Nyerere praised their go-ahead spirit but suggested obliquely that there was also virtue in giving a system time to prove itself before embarking on a new one.

Personally, I think the future belongs to those who, like the Wachagga, are ready to take in new ideas. Like all with open minds they will take in a lot of rubbish. They will certainly not be a tourist attraction. But in the end, life will favor those who come to terms with it, not those who run away. I was not surprised to find that, although the Wachagga had no tradition of art, they have produced East Africa's best-known painter, Sam Ntiro, and one of its best sculptors. Neither was I surprised to meet a Chagga in Moshi who was working, with a devotion that would earn credit in the Academy of Lagado, on a new script written from the bottom of the page to the top!

The Warlike Wahehe

Anyone who is familiar with Nigeria knows about the passenger lorries, or mammy wagons, and of the legends for which they are famed. Sometimes the inscriptions are self-explanatory, for example: They Say, Let

Them Say; Salutation Is Not Love; No Telephone to Heaven, etc. But once in a while you do come across a truly esoteric legend. On my way to and from school at the end of the Second World War, I used often to see a lorry with such a name; just one word: WAHEHE. Had it anything to do with laughter? I wondered. But its inscrutable name notwithstanding, WAHEHE was a most popular lorry on the Enugu-Onitsha road. Whenever it came along children greeted it with loud cries of Wahehe! Wahehe!

So when in December 1960 I heard in Tanganyika of a tribe by that name, I decided immediately to visit their country.

In the last century the Wahehe were great warriors with an astonishing record which included the defeat of the much celebrated Masai but also of the colonizing Germans, more ruthless in battle than even the Masai. When the story of African resistance to European subjugation comes to be written, the military exploits of Sultan Mkwawa of the Wahehe will be given prominence and honor.

Mkwawa became chief in 1880. Within a few years he had subdued all the troublesome peoples in the surrounding country and raised the reputation of Wahehe warriors to unprecedented heights. It is said that on hearing of a Masai invasion Sultan Mkwawa, in demonstration of his contempt, sent his sister at the head of his forces which totally routed the invaders.

Unknown to Mkwawa his territory had fallen to the Germans in the great European scramble for Africa. So when the Germans arrived to pacify their new possession, Mkwawa failed to see the need for that particular blessing and remained intransigent. The Germans immediately sent a strong expeditionary force of 1,000 troops to teach him a sharp lesson. Sultan Mkwawa ambushed the invading army and inflicted such heavy casualties on them that they only narrowly escaped complete annihilation. Shocked and humiliated, the Germans took three years to prepare another expedition. This time they sent well over five companies.

Meanwhile Mkwawa was using the three-year respite to fortify his kingdom. He was building a stone wall eight miles in circumference round his capital, using for this work anyone proved cowardly in battle. Unfortunately this gigantic undertaking was still unfinished when the Germans struck again. With their immensely superior armament, they easily conquered the Wahehe army. But they discovered to their great annoyance that they had practically to subdue every hut separately and yet were unable to capture Mkwawa on whose head a large reward had been placed. For three long years more he eluded them. Then one day a young officer, going into the forest to investigate a shot that had been heard, found the Sultan's body. He had shot himself rather than surrender and be taken prisoner. The young officer cut off the head and took it to headquarters in Iringa and a reward of 5,000 rupees was paid over to him.

The Germans who seemed to have a curious taste in these matters dried the head and sent it to a museum in the fatherland. It was not until 1954, almost seventy years later, that a British governor of Tanganyika, realizing how much the Wahehe still suffered from the trauma of that event, made moves to recover Mkwawa's head. It was a long and morbid story. But in the end Mkwawa's skull was identified from among two thousand others in a museum in Bremen and returned to Chief Adam Sapi, Sultan

Mkwawa's grandson, at a solemn ceremony watched in silence by thousands of Wahehe people.

Chief Adam Sapi does not look at all warlike. He is quiet and totally unassuming. But perhaps Sultan Mkwawa himself would have looked peaceful and unassuming in 1960, having seen his territory overrun first by the Germans and then by the British and now hearing rumors of independence, albeit of a different kind. Strangely enough, Adam Sapi's father (and son of Mkwawa) was deposed by the British administration during the Second World War for alleged pro-German sympathies! And Adam Sapi, then hardly more than a boy, was brought home from Makerere College to assume the chieftaincy.

I had the honor of being invited to tea by Chief Sapi. He wore a smart lounge suit and after tea drove me furiously in his Mercedes car to see the new house he was building. The next morning as I was packing my bag to return to Dar es Salaam someone knocked on my hotel door. It was Chief Sapi come to make me a present of a miniature Wahehe spear. I was greatly moved and flattered by such attention from the grandson of the great Sultan Mkwawa.

Now, how did the name of his people find itself on a lorry in Nigeria in the forties when there was so little contact between East and West Africa? I have discovered that a few Nigerian soldiers fought under the British in Tanganyika in the two wars. Perhaps one of them liked the sound of that name and took it home, but we cannot be sure. Which actually pleases me, for I like a residue of mystery always to remain. After my visit, the strange legend I had seen as a child on that lorry lost its magic.

And although the visit had been truly rewarding, I had mixed feelings about my loss. As we always should when a familiar sense of wonder and innocence departs and knowledge settles in.

1961

THE AFRICAN WRITER AND THE BIAFRAN CAUSE[1]

The point which this paper will be making really amounts to this: that the involvement of the Biafran writer today in the cause for which his people are fighting and dying is not different from the involvement of many African writers—past and present—in the big issues of Africa. The fact of war merely puts the matter in sharper focus.

It is clear to me that an African creative writer who tries to avoid the big social and political issues of contemporary Africa will end up being completely irrelevant —like that absurd man in the proverb who leaves his burning house to pursue a rat fleeing from the flames. And let no one tell me that if this was true for African writers, it must also be true for others. The fact is that some of the great issues of Africa have never been issues at all,

[1] A paper read at a political science seminar at Makerere University College, Kampala, Uganda, on August 25, 1968, at the height of the Biafran War. Fortunately some of the details are dated but not, unfortunately, the central argument.

or else have ceased to be important for, say, Europeans. Take for instance the issue of racial inequality which—whether or not we realize it—is at the very root of Africa's problems and has been for four hundred years. It has become fashionable to beguile ourselves into believing that all "reasonable" people accept the idea of human equality and that the minority who do not accept it are mentally sick and will be cured in due course.

To take this comforting view is regarded as being level-headed and civilized. To keep hammering at racial insult is extremist and tiresome and may even show racism in reverse. We all know the little joke of the African in London who ordered coffee and then stormed out of the restaurant when he was asked "white or black." To be able to make such jokes against ourselves is of course a most welcome sign of self-confidence. Obviously it would be a ridiculous waste of energy to go through life fighting imaginary insults. At the same time, to go through life swallowing real insults is to compromise one's self-respect. Whether we like to face up to it or not, Africa has been the most insulted continent in the world. Africans' very claim to humanity has been questioned at various times, their persons abused, their intelligence insulted. These things have happened in the past and have gone on happening tòday. We have a duty to bring them to an end for our own sakes, for the sake of our children, and indeed for the safety and happiness of the world. And "we" includes writers.

In the last four hundred years, Africa has been menaced by Europe. We may break these four centuries into three important periods:
   a) the slave trade
   b) colonization
   c) decolonization

During these three periods, the inherent assumptions of Europe with regard to Africa have not changed as much as we like to think. Admittedly if a John Hawkins were to fit out a slave ship from Plymouth today, he would be universally condemned. The world would not stand for it. That much progress must be conceded. But let us look beyond Hawkins' action to his basic assumptions. We will find there a belief that the slave is somewhat less than human. Whether we like to admit it or not, this kind of belief is not entirely obsolete. It certainly was present (no doubt in a somewhat attenuated form) in colonization. No one arrogates to himself the right to order the lives of a whole people unless he takes for granted his own superiority over those people. European colonizers of Africa had no difficulty in taking their own superiority for granted. Neither do their present descendants (and this includes America and Russia) who set out to manipulate emergent Africa.

This assumption of superiority becomes particularly dangerous when—as in our case—it gets mixed up with color and race.

How then does all this affect the writer?

If an artist is anything, he is a human being with heightened sensitivities; he must be aware of the faintest nuances of injustice in human relations. The African writer cannot therefore be unaware of, or indifferent to, the monumental injustice which his people suffer. Among the very earliest African writers in English was an ex-slave, Olauda Equiano, who called himself Gustavus Vassa, the African. In his most remarkable autobiography,[2] published in London in 1789, one of his primary concerns was to do battle against those fundamental as-

2 *The Interesting Narrative of Olauda Equiano, or Gustavus Vassa, the African* (2 vols.). London, 1789. Editor

sumptions of which I speak. Equiano described with great
feeling and longing the simple beauty of his half-
remembered African childhood. "We are almost a nation
of dancers, musicians and poets," he wrote. In another
place he said, "Our women too were, in my eyes at least,
uncommonly graceful." I suppose he had to put in that
subjective qualification—in my eyes at least—to make the
thing at all plausible—so unpropitious were his times. It
must have taken a lot of courage to fight that lonely battle
in London in 1789. In taking the colorful name of Gustavus Vassa, the African, Equiano no doubt sought to bring
to his cause the magic and success of the Swedish patriot
who led his people to freedom.

(I might add with pride and no chauvinism, I hope,
that Olauda Equiano was born in the first half of the
eighteenth century in that part of West Africa called
Biafra today.)

Equiano then represents the African writer's response
to Europe's first assault on the life and dignity of Africans
during the period of the slave trade.

Let us now turn to the middle period—one might almost
say the middle passage—which saw the colonization of
Africa by alien races. While few people today would try
to defend the slave-trade period, there are apologists who
will point to the many benefits which came to Africa in
the wake of colonization. For instance, the foundations
of future nation-states were laid, Africa was introduced
to the arts of civilization and given the true religion, etc.
These arguments need not detain us as they are hardly
relevant to the main point I am making. I am concerned
here with the underlying attitudes of people to people.
If the attitudes are wrong, then a whole lot of other things
go awry. Depending on how it is given, a gift could be-

come an insult, and a juicy morsel turn to gall. A giver's face is eaten, says a proverb, before the gift in his hand.

What then were the underlying attitudes of the European colonizer to Africa and its people? In 1884 European statesmen met in Berlin and simply divided the land of the blacks among themselves. The blacks were of course divided alongside the land on which they stood. Then one fine morning, Queen Victoria remembered her cousin the Kaiser's birthday and gave him Tanganyika with many happy returns!

Arrogance, contempt, levity—these were some of the attitudes. That great imperial poet Kipling called the African "half devil, half child."

There is a touch of almost disarming levity in all this. But it has its serious moments too when the "blond beast" bares its ivory teeth and the white latex of the Congo rubber turns red.

"The white man killed my father," cried David Diop.
"My father was strong.
The white man raped my mother.
My mother was beautiful."

But most African writers adopted a more moderate tone—a tone of almost sweet reasonableness, reminiscent of Equiano.

They call us cotton heads and
coffee men and oily men.
They call us men of death.
But we are men of the dance
Whose feet only gain power
When they beat the hard soil.

That was Senghor, of course. But even he could on occasion be overwhelmed by the wickedness and hypocrisy of Europe, of diplomats who today will still barter with black flesh.

Our prose writers were naturally concerned with the same basic issues, but on the whole adopted a more conciliatory tone—no violent accusations of murder and rape. The attitude of the writer seemed to be that once a good case had been made for his people's culture and institutions, the rest could be left to the good sense of the reader. A common criticism of this genre of African protest writing is that it was addressed to Europeans. This is mostly true and I do not see how it could have been otherwise. After all it was Europe which introduced into Africa the problems which the writer was attempting to solve. But it is not entirely true that these writings were addressed solely to the European reader. The writer was also trying to restore to his people a good opinion of themselves because their association with Europe had visibly undermined their self-confidence. Dr. Emmanuel Obiechina is right when he sees in West African writing ". . . a purpose, implicit or explicit, to correct the distortions of the West African culture, to recreate the past in the present in order to educate the West African reader and give him confidence in his cultural heritage, and also in order to enlighten the foreign reader and help him get rid of the false impressions about the West African culture acquired from centuries of cultural misrepresentation."

The third phase of Europe-Africa relationships opened just over ten years ago with the independence of Ghana. "Seek ye first the political kingdom," said Nkrumah, "and all other things will be added unto you."

In Nigeria the national freedom movement created a freedom song:

> Freedom, freedom
> Everywhere there will be freedom!
> Freedom for you and freedom for me
> Everywhere there will be freedom!

And we sang it to a swinging, evangelical-hymn tune from *Sacred Songs and Solos*. And danced it until our feet gained power beating the hard soil. And Europe capitulated. Or so we thought. In the words of Dr. Nnamdi Azikiwe, Nigeria was given her freedom "on a platter of gold." Like the head of John the Baptist, this gift to Nigeria proved most unlucky. The British, who had done precious little to create a spirit of common nationality in Nigeria during the fifty years they were in control, made certain on the eve of their departure that power went to that conservative element in the country which had played no part in the struggle for independence. This would insure Nigeria's obedience even unto freedom. As a first sign of this, the British High Commissioner took up residence next door to the Prime Minister who was of course a British knight.

Within six years of independence, Nigeria was a cesspool of corruption and misrule. Public servants helped themselves freely to the nation's wealth. A certain professor has recently described the government of many African countries as a kleptocracy. Nigeria could certainly be called that. Elections were blatantly rigged. (One British weekly captioned its story of a Nigerian election NIGERRIMANDERING.) The national census was outrageously stage-managed; judges and magistrates were manipulated by politicians in power. The politicians themselves were manipulated and corrupted by foreign business interests.

This was the situation in which I wrote *A Man of the People*. The irrepressible Wole Soyinka put on the stage a devastating satire, *Before the Black-out,* which played to packed houses night after night in Ibadan. The popular traveling theater of Hubert Ogunde and his many wives began to stage a play clearly directed against the crooked premier of Western Nigeria. The theater group was declared an unlawful society and banned in that region. Things were coming to a head. After an unbelievable election swindle, violence erupted as a result of the anger and frustration of Western Nigerians. It was in these circumstances that Wole Soyinka was charged with holding up Ibadan radio station and removing the premier's taped speech!

The Prime Minister of Nigeria who had been built up into a great statesman by the Western press did nothing to save his country from impending chaos. Yet he found time to call a Commonwealth Conference in Lagos to discuss Rhodesia and to save his good friend Harold Wilson from the consequences of an OAU resolution to which Nigeria had subscribed.

The point I want to make here is that the creative writer in independent Nigeria found himself with a new, terrifying problem on his hands. He found that the independence his country was supposed to have won was totally without content. The old white master was still in power. He had got himself a bunch of black stooges to do his dirty work for a commission. As long as they did what was expected of them they would be praised for their sagacity and their country for its stability.

As everyone knows, Nigeria was upset in January 1966

by five young army majors. Nigerians were wild with joy at the fall of the corrupt and hated governments of the federation. Britain writhed in pain. It is said that the British intelligence service in Nigeria was rebuked and completely reorganized.

Meanwhile the story got around that the military coup which had been so well received was in fact a sinister plot by the ambitious Ibos of the east to seize control of Nigeria. In a country in which tribalism was endemic this interpretation did not wait too long to find acceptance. Many people were quickly persuaded that their spontaneous jubilation in January had been a mistake. A little later it became a fact that only the Ibos had rejoiced. A Nigerian poet, who had dedicated a new book "to the heroes of January 1966," had second thoughts after the countercoup of July and sent a frantic cable to his publishers to remove the dedication.

The story of the massacre of thousands of innocent Eastern Nigerians need not be retold here. But a few of its salient features should be recalled. First it was a carefully planned operation. Secondly it has never been condemned by the Nigerian government. In short, thousands of citizens were slaughtered, hundreds of thousands were wounded and maimed and violated, their homes and property looted and burned; and no one asked any questions. A Sierra Leonian living in Northern Nigeria at the time wrote in horror: "The killing of the Ibos has become a state industry in Nigeria."

> The white man killed my father
> My father was strong
> The white man raped my mother
> My mother was beautiful.

David Diop unfortunately died too young. He would have known that the black man can also murder and rape. Wole Soyinka, if he is alive,[3] knows it. Christopher Okigbo, though he too died young, lived long enough to know it.

Biafra stands in opposition to the murder and rape of Africa by whites and blacks alike because she has tasted both and found them equally bitter. No government, black or white, has the right to stigmatize and destroy groups of its own citizens without undermining the basis of its own existence. The government of Nigeria failed to protect the fourteen million people of its former Eastern Nigeria from wanton destruction and rightly lost their allegiance.

Secondly, Biafra stands for true independence in Africa, for an end to the four hundred years of shame and humiliation which we have suffered in our association with Europe. Britain knows this and is using Nigeria to destroy Biafra.

"We hope to found a single federal Nigeria," said a British minister in parliament on February 13, 1968. One may ask, What business has Britain to found anything at this late hour in an African country which is sovereign and independent? Only last Wednesday an editorial in the *Financial Times* carried these words:

> It is appropriate that the leader of the Nigerian delegation to the Peace Talks, Chief Anthony Enahoro, should choose this moment to be not in Ethiopia but in London where he has been having talks with the British government. He will have been telling Lord

---

[3] There were rumors at this time that Soyinka had died in prison.

Shepherd, the Minister of State, of the reasons for the
failure of the negotiations. . . .

That is Nigerian independence. Biafran writers are committed to the revolutionary struggle of their people for
justice and true independence. Gabriel Okara, Cyprian
Ekwensi, Onuora Nzekwu, Nkem Nwankwo, John Mu-
nonye, V. C. Ike, Flora Nwapa are all working actively in
this cause for which Christopher Okigbo died. I believe
our cause is right and just. And this is what literature in
Africa should be about today—right and just causes.

1968

DEAR TAI SOLARIN

Dear Tai Solarin,

On October 20 in your weekly *Daily Times* column you made what I call an unwarranted attack on me. You wrote as follows:

> It is sickening reading Chinua Achebe defending English as our lingua franca. I do not blame Achebe or any other Nigerian novelist taking the same stand. Their books are, commercially speaking, necessarily written in English.

Those are indeed potent words worthy of close attention. It is unlikely that many of your readers will have seen my article to which you referred. So I should begin by explaining to them what I did say since you were obviously too sickened to comprehend it.

It is not necessary for me, or anybody else for that matter, to rush to the defense of English in Nigeria: it seems

more than able to defend itself. What I was concerned
with was to pin-point the historical reasons for the as-
cendancy of English today and to suggest ways in which
our imaginative writers *who choose* to write in it might
enrich their idiom and imagery by drawing from their
own traditional sources. So much for your first sentence.

The second and third sentences go on to suggest that
since my books are written in English I have a financial interest in defending its use in Nigeria. Very clever, but I'm
afraid not clever enough. Have you not heard of translations? My novels are not only in English but in sixteen
major languages around the world. And the number is
increasing. I am quite confident that if Nigeria decided
tomorrow to install Hausa as the national language my
books would immediately be translated into it. So, you
see, I need not fear such an event. Financially I might
even be the better off for it!

But may I ask you one little question? If you are truly as
sickened by a defense of English as you make out, why
have you gone on week after week, year after year, in
season and out of it, writing and publishing your newspaper column in the same loathsome language? Surely,
Hausa or Yoruba or Igbo should have been the obvious
medium for you. The very article I am complaining about
runs to well over a thousand words, which means that in
the course of one year you publish over fifty thousand
words in the *Daily Times* (to say nothing of your pam-
phleteering). Do you realize that all that verbiage is
equivalent in quantity if not merit to a full-length novel?
Now, this is a lot more than I or any other Nigerian novelist dare inflict on the reading public. You are on this evi-

dence what Nkem Nwankwo would call "a voracious writer"—in English. And yet you are sickened by my "defense" of it. Have you acquired the dog's facility for being sick, throwing up, and then returning to eat the vomit?

And I guess the *Daily Times* pays you for throwing up this weekly mess which (to borrow your own phrase) is "commercially speaking necessarily" thrown up in English.

Now let us take a quick look at *your* defense of Hausa. Isn't it incredible that anybody outside a mental asylum should choose a time such as this[1] to urge "the Nigerian Army" (which one, by the way?) to impose Hausa on the country? It is unlikely that anyone will take any notice of your proposal, but making it has portrayed you as an unfeeling, dry-as-dust logic chopper with no capacity at all for respecting human anguish; as concerned as ever with sounding clever and "revolutionary" rather than seeing any problems solved.

Which immediately brings to mind a truly sickening article of yours I read as a student in the fifties—a strange apologia for Adolf Hitler. As you are so anxious to shock people and seem to be a little short of ideas, why don't you fish out that article and publish it again? It is guaranteed to shock your new friends in Israel.

But to return to Nigeria. You say that if we had all been taught Hausa instead of English fifty years ago, we would not have experienced "May and August." That is an "if"

[1] Thousands of Ibos were massacred in the Hausa north of Nigeria in May, August, and September 1966.

of history. The fact is that we were not taught Hausa for the rather obvious reason that the makers and rulers of Nigeria were not Hausa but English. To choose October 1966 to regret this fact is foolish and irresponsible. In your grand designs for Nigeria do not discount human beings: it will get us nowhere.

In conclusion let me acknowledge in fairness to you that you did make one grudging concession to reality when you wrote (albeit in rather unfelicitous prose) that your suggestion to impose Hausa on the country "must be painful thought to the widowed mother with two sick children with the father lost in Kano or Jos. . . ." May I remind you that in all likelihood that widow and her sick (wounded?) children do, and her dead husband did, speak excellent Hausa and little English.

Yours sincerely,

Chinua Achebe.

(Published in the *Daily Times*, Lagos, November 7, 1966)

ONITSHA, GIFT OF THE NIGER

In the ten years since Mr. Ulli Beier first drew the attention of the outside world to the amazing pamphlet literature of the Onitsha market in the *Times Literary Supplement*, a good many scholarly studies of it have been made and published. This is as it should be, for it is indeed a phenomenon of consuming interest whether we view it as literature or as sociology.

One of the most intriguing questions concerning this literature—Why did it happen in Onitsha?—has, however, not yet been answered fully and I suspect never will be. For when all the geographical, historical, social-political, economic, and all the other rational explanations have been given for a truly unique phenomenon, there will always remain an area of shadows where some (at least) of the truth will seek to hide. It is this area which interests me—the esoteric region from which creativity sallies forth at will to manifest itself. All we can do is to speculate. Onitsha is such a phenomenon. Whenever I think of it, a phrase from Frantz Fanon comes immediately to my mind: *a zone of occult instability*.

In its 2,600-mile journey from the Futa Jalon Moun-
tains through savannahs, scrublands, and desert and then
southward through tropical forests, finally losing itself in
a thousand digressions in the Bight of Biafra, the River
Niger sees many lands and diverse human settlements,
old and new, picturesque and ordinary: Goa and Tim-
buktu of medieval fame; Lokoja created by British zeal-
ots of "legitimate commerce" one hundred years ago and
ridiculed by a skeptical Charles Dickens as so much
"Borrio-boola-Gha"; Bussa, passive witness of an explor-
er's disaster in 1805, now itself sunk beneath the waters
of a gargantuan hydroelectric lake. By the time the River
Niger gets to Onitsha, it has answered many names, seen
a multitude of sights; it is now big, experienced, and un-
hurried. Its name is simply *Orimili* or plenitude of waters.

Onitsha is an Igbo town which claims Benin origin. If
we are to believe historians, this claim is not very well
founded. But what really matters is that Onitsha *feels* different from the peoples and places in its vicinity. And it
is different. It sits at the crossroads of the world. It has
two faces—a Benin face and an Igbo face—and can see
the four directions; either squarely or with the tail of an
eye. Its market, which had assembled originally on one of
the four days of the Igbo week, had likewise grown "big
eyes" and engulfed every day in the sky, and become
(before its destruction in the Biafran War) the biggest
and most spectacular market in the whole world.

Because it sees everything, Onitsha has come to dis-
trust single-mindedness. It can be opposite things at
once. It was both a cradle of Christianity in Igboland
and a veritable fortress of "pagan" revanchism. Many hinterland peoples who received the first light of the gospel
from Onitsha converts soon became more zealous than

their teachers and would often say with a sad shake of the head that an Onitsha man had too much of the world in him to make a good Christian.

There is a story about one of the earliest converts in Onitsha at the turn of the century who did so well in the new faith that the Church Missionary Society decided to send him to England for higher studies and ordination. While in England he quickly lost the faith that took him there and returned to Onitsha where he obstructed the work of evangelization by his nefarious example. Why did the church preach so vehemently against heathen titles, he asked? What were all those knights and barons and dukes if not hierarchies of *ozo*? He took all the titles he could find and died a pagan.

But then there was also another Onitsha man, the Venerable Archdeacon Nweje, a saint and divine whose sometimes quixotic acts of holiness and other-worldliness are recounted to this day: who once surprised a thief digging up his yams but was less distressed by that than the possibility of the man hurting himself in his reckless flight through the forest of spiky yam stakes. Stop! You will hurt yourself! Come and take some of the yams! he called out in vain.

Onitsha was always the marketplace of the world. In its ancient emporium the people of Olu and Igbo—the riverain folk and the dwellers of the hinterland forests—met in guarded, somewhat uneasy, commerce; old-time farmers met new, urban retail traders of known and outlandish wares. Onitsha was the original site of evangelical dialogue between proselytizing Christianity and Igbo religion; between strange-looking toeless harbingers of white rule and (at first) an amused and indulgent black population that assembled in their hundreds to enjoy the alien spectacle. It was finally the occult no man's land between river spirits and mundane humans.

Onitsha had always attracted the exceptional, the colorful and the bizarre because it was itself colorful and bizarre. My mother told me of a madman who went to Onitsha long, long ago and found it immensely bewildering. Back in his village he told how everything there was blind (everything of the white man, that is) and proceeded to count off on his fingers: office, police, matches, Alice, notice.[1] At about the same time there was a strange Englishman living in Onitsha—J. M. Stuart-Young—scholar, mystic, trader, singlehanded fighter against the new European monopolistic cartels. He was a legend among the Igbo even in his lifetime; for was he not a lover of the wealth-giving but fiendishly jealous mermaid-queen of the Niger River? They called him Eke (python) which he disliked and Odeziaku (Arranger of Wealth) which he didn't. He was a mystery man and nothing is known for certain about his life before he fell like a comet into Onitsha. . . . He said he was a doctor of philosophy, and perhaps he was.

There was a half-mad minstrel called Okoli Ukpor whom I remember with the memory of childhood. If you went to Onitsha in those days and did not run into Okoli, your visit was somehow incomplete. He played for money on his flute, whistling and blowing his instrument alternately: "Man and woman, whoever holds money, let him bring!" Clearly not much of a lyric; but how appropriate to his day! Occasionally he would raise an additional laugh and an additional half penny by blowing each nostril in turn into the open drain—in time with his beat. Rumor had it that Okoli was as sober as the next man, that

[1] Each of these words ends in *isi* which means blindness.

he had two wives and a barnful of yams in his hinterland home and only came down to Onitsha during the slack moments in the farm to raise quick cash from amused charity by pretending to be lightheaded. If that was true (and even if it wasn't), where else would such as he go but to Onitsha where the simple mutual-trust village economy was yielding place to a new, somewhat intoxicating, somewhat unscrupulous, cash nexus?

Onitsha was the nursery of a burgeoning Igbo capitalism—a capitalism tempered albeit by the still strong traditional kindred concerns of the extended family and by the leveling mechanism in Igbo culture tempting and inducing a man to hand back his capital to his people in return for titles and decorations.

Onitsha was a place of schools—day schools and night schools, mission schools and private schools, grammar schools and commercial institutes, a city of one-room academies and backyard colleges. It had the best, the indifferent, and the deplorable. Its major industry was retail trading and the next was education, and the two sometimes got mixed up. Onitsha was a self-confident place where a man would not be deterred, even by insufficient learning, from aspiring to teach and improve his fellows—and making a little profit as well.

(This essay in a shorter form was published as foreword to Dr. Obiechina's *An African Popular Literature.* University Press, 1973.)

CHI IN IGBO[1] COSMOLOGY

There are two clearly distinct meanings of the word *chi* in Igbo. The first is often translated as god, guardian angel, personal spirit, soul, spirit double, etc. The second meaning is day, or daylight, but is most commonly used for those transitional periods between day and night or night and day. Thus we speak of *chi ofufo* meaning daybreak and *chi ojiji,* nightfall. We also have the word *mgbachi* for that most potent hour of noon that splits the day in two, a time favored in folklore by itinerant spirits and feared by children.

I am chiefly concerned here with the first meaning of chi, a concept so central in Igbo psychology and yet so elusive and enigmatic. The great variety of words and phrases which has been put forward at different times by different people as translations of this concept attests to its great complexity and lends additional force to the

[1] The Igbo people (called Ibo by the English) inhabit southeastern Nigeria. They caught world attention for a while as chief protagonists of the Biafran tragedy. Igbo is both the people (about ten million) and their language.

famous plea of Dr. J. B. Danquah that we pay one another's gods the compliment of calling them by their proper name.

In a general way we may visualize a person's chi as his other identity in spiritland—his *spirit being* complementing his terrestrial *human being;* for nothing can stand alone, there must always be another thing standing beside it.

Without an understanding of the nature of chi one could not begin to make sense of the Igbo world-view; and yet no study of it exists that could even be called preliminary. What I am attempting here is not to fill that gap but to draw attention to it in a manner appropriate to one whose primary love is literature and not religion, philosophy, or linguistics. I will not even touch upon such tantalizing speculations as what happens to a person's chi when the person dies and its shrine is destroyed. Does it retreat completely back to its old home? And finally what happens at the man's reincarnation?

But before we embark on a consideration of the nature and implication of this concept which is so powerful in Igbo religion and thought, let us examine briefly what connection there may be between it and the other meaning of chi. For a long time I was convinced that there couldn't possibly be any relationship between chi (spirit being) and chi (daylight) except as two words that just happened to sound alike. But one day I stumbled on the very important information that among the Igbo of Awka a man who has arrived at the point in his life when he needs to set up a shrine to his chi will invite a priest to perform a ritual of bringing down the spirit from the face of the sun at daybreak. Thereafter it is represented physically in the man's compound until the day of his death when the shrine must be destroyed.

The implication of this is that a person's chi normally resides with the sun, bringer of daylight, or at least passes through it to visit the world. Which itself may have an even profounder implication, for it is well known in Igbo cosmology that the Supreme Deity, Chukwu Himself, is in close communion with the sun. But more on that later.

Since Igbo people did not construct a rigid and closely argued system of thought to explain the universe and the place of man in it, preferring the metaphor of myth and poetry, anyone seeking an insight into their world must seek it along their own way. Some of these ways are folk tales, proverbs, proper names, rituals, and festivals. There is of course the "scientific" way as well—the tape-recorded interview with old people. Unfortunately it is often more impressive than useful. The old people who have the information we seek will not often bare their hearts to any passer-by. They will give answers, and true answers too. But there is truth and there is truth. To get to the inner truth will often require more time than the recording interviewer can give—it may require a whole lifetime. In any case no one talks naturally into a strange box of tricks!

It is important to stress what I said earlier: the central place in Igbo thought of the notion of duality. Wherever Something stands, Something Else will stand beside it. Nothing is absolute. *I am the truth, the way, and the life* would be called blasphemous or simply absurd, for is it not well known that a man may worship Ogwugwu to perfection and yet be killed by Udo? The world in which we live has its double and counterpart in the realm of spirits. A man lives here and his chi there. Indeed the human being is only one half (and the weaker half at that) of a person. There is a complementary spirit being, chi. (The word *spirit*, though useful, does create serious problems of its own, however, for it is used to describe many different orders of non-human being.) Thus the abode of chi may be confused with *ani mmo* where the dead who encounter no obstacles in their passage go to live. But ani mmo is thought to be not above, like the realm of chi, but below, inside the earth. Considerable confusion and obscurity darken the picture at this point because there is a sense in which the two supernatural worlds are both seen as parallel to the land of the living. In an early anthropological study of the Igbo, Major A. G. Leonard at the opening of this century reported the following account from one of his Igbo informants:

> We Ibo look forward to the next world as being much the same as this . . . we picture life there to be exactly as it is in this world. The ground there is just the same as it is here; the earth is similar. There are forests and hills and valleys with rivers flowing and roads leading from one town to another. . . . People in spiritland have their ordinary occupations, the farmer his farm.[2]

This "spiritland" where dead ancestors recreate a life comparable to their earthly existence is not only parallel to the human world but is also similar and physically contiguous with it, for there is constant coming and going between them in the endless traffic of life, death, and reincarnation. The masked spirits who often grace human rituals and ceremonies with their presence are repre-

[2] A. G. Leonard, *The Lower Niger and Its Tribes.* London: Cass, pp. 185–86.

sentative visitors from this underworld and are said to emerge from their subterranean home through ant holes. At least that is the story as told to the uninitiated. To those who know, however, the masked "spirits" are only *symbolic* ancestors. But this knowledge does not in any way diminish their validity or the awesomeness of their presence.

These ancestral spirits which may be personified by man are, however, of a very different order from chi and so is their place of abode. There is a story of how a proud wrestler, having thrown every challenger in the world, decides to go and wrestle in the world of spirits. There he also throws challenger after challenger, including many multiple-headed ones—so great was his prowess. At last there is no one left to fight. But the wrestler refuses to leave. The spirits beg him to go; his companion praise-singer on the flute pleads with him. But it is all in vain. *There must be somebody left; surely the famed land of spirits can do better than this,* he said. Again everyone begs him to collect his laurels and go, but again he refuses. Finally his own chi appears, reluctant, thin as a rope. The wrestler laughs at this miserable-looking contender and moves forward contemptuously to knock him down, whereupon the other lifts him clear off the ground with his little finger and smashes him to death.

This cautionary tale is concerned mainly, I think, with setting a limit to man's aspirations. The limit is not the sky; it is somewhere much closer to earth. A sensible man will turn round at the frontiers of absolutism and head for home again. There is, however, around the story as well a vague intimation that the place where chi inhabits is forbidden to man in a way that ani mmo, the abode of his dead fathers, does not appear to be. For we have, at least, a description of the landscape of ani mmo; nothing comparable exists for the territory of chi.

There is another cautionary tale about chi, this time involving the little bird, *nza*, who ate and drank somewhat more than was good for him and in a fit of recklessness, which inebriation alone would explain, taunted his chi to come and get him if he could. Whereupon a hawk swooped down from the clear sky and carried him away. Which shows the foolishness of counting on chi's remoteness, for chi need not come in person or act directly but may use one's enemy who is close by.

The story of the headstrong wrestler, in addition to all the other things it tells us, makes also the important point that a man's chi does have a special hold over him such as no other powers can muster. This is why, for instance, it can dispense with the physical endowments and terrors of the multiple-headed spirits. This special power that chi has over its man (or the man's special vulnerability to his chi) is further exemplified in a proverb: *No matter how many divinities sit together to plot a man's ruin, it will come to nothing unless his chi is there among them.* Clearly chi has unprecedented veto powers over a man's destiny.

But power so complete, even in the hands of chi, is abhorrent to the Igbo imagination. Therefore the makers of proverbs went to work again, as it were, to create others that would set a limit to its exercise. Hence the well-known *Onye kwe chie ekwe.* (If a man agrees, his chi agrees.) And so the initiative, or some of it at least, is returned to man.

If you want to know how life has treated an Igbo man, a good place to look is the names his children bear. His hopes, his fears, his joys and sorrows; his grievances against his fellows, or complaints about the way he has been used by fortune; even straight historical records are all there. And because chi is so central to Igbo thought, we will also find much about it in proper names—more I think than from any other single source.

Chika (chi is supreme); Chibuzo (chi is in front); Nebechi (look to chi) are only a few examples of the large number of names that show the general primacy of chi over mankind. Chinwuba asserts chi's special responsibility for increase and prosperity; Chinwendu, its power over life; and Chikadibia, over health. A man who suffers from false accusations or calumnies heaped on him by his fellows may call his child Chiebonam (may chi not accuse me) meaning that the moral justification which chi can give is what counts in the end. It is, however, unusual to link chi in this way with moral sanction, a responsibility that belongs normally to Ani, the earth goddess and proper source of moral law—a fact recognized in the name Aniebonam which is analogous to Chiebonam.

The Igbo believe that a man receives his gifts or talents, his character—indeed his portion in life generally—before he comes into the world. It seems there is an element of choice available to him at that point, and that his chi presides over the bargaining. Hence the saying *Obu etu nya na chie si kwu*, which we often hear when a man's misfortune is somehow beyond comprehension and so can only be attributable to an agreement he himself must have entered into, at the beginning, alone with his chi; for there is a fundamental justice in the universe and nothing so terrible can happen to a person for which he is not somehow responsible. A few other names suggest this role of chi as the great dealer out of gifts: Nkechinyelu and Chijioke, for example.

Although, as we have seen, the Igbo believe that when a man says yes his chi will also agree; but not always. Sometimes a man may struggle with all his power and say yes most emphatically and yet nothing he attempts will succeed. Quite simply the Igbo say of such a man: *Chie ekwero*. (His chi does not agree.) Now, this could mean one of two things; either the man has a particularly intransigent chi or else it is the man himself attempting too late to alter that primordial bargain he had willingly struck with his chi, saying yes now when his first unalterable word had been no, forgetting that "the first word gets to Chukwu's house."

But of course the idea of an intransigent chi does exist in Igbo: *ajo chi*, literally *bad chi*. We must remember, however, when we hear that a man has a bad chi that we are talking about his fortune rather than his character. A man of impeccable character may yet have a bad chi so that nothing he puts his hand to will work out right. Chi is therefore more concerned with success or failure than with righteousness and wickedness. Which is not to say that it is totally indifferent to morality. For we should know by now that nothing is *totally* anything in Igbo thinking; everything is a question of measure and degree. We have already seen in the name Chiebonam that chi shares a little of the moral concerns of Ani, the earth goddess. But in addition there is a hint of moral attribution to chi in the way the Igbo sometimes explain differences in human character. For maximum dramatization they pick two brothers who are dissimilar in character: one good, the other bad. And they say: *Ofu nne n'amu, ma ofu chi adeke*, a very neat and tight statement which can only be approximately interpreted as: one mother gives birth, different chi create.

This statement apart from reiterating the idea of "one man, one chi" goes further to introduce the fundamental notion of chi as creator which is of the utmost importance: a man does not only have his own chi but is created by it and no two people, not even blood brothers, it seems, are created by the same chi. What we know of chi can thus be summed up as follows: every person has an individual chi who created him; its natural home is somewhere in the region of the sun, but it may be induced to visit an earthly shrine; a person's fortunes in life are controlled more or less completely by his chi. (Perhaps this is a good place to point out that there are many minor, and occasionally even major, divergences of perception about chi from different parts of Igbo land so that one can at best only follow what appears to be the dominant and persistent concepts. For example, although communities exist which assert categorically that chi lives with Chukwu, in most places such closeness can only be deduced indirectly.)

There are many names and sayings in Igbo which confirm the creative role of chi. When we name a child Chiekezie, we imply that chi has restored a certain balance by that particular creation, or has at last apportioned shares equitably. Of a man unattractive or deficient in character, we might say: *Chi ya kegbulu ya ekegbu.* Here again there are two possible interpretations to our statement: either the man in question was created badly or else was cheated of his full share of things. Or both interpretations may even be intended, for what else is creation but the imparting of distinguishing characteristics and bestowing of gifts? Certainly the Igbo language by having the same root word *ke* for *create* and *share* does encourage this notion.

The idea of individualism is sometimes traced to the Christian principle that God created all men and consequently every one of them is presumed worthy in His sight. The Igbo do better than that. They postulate the concept of every man as both a unique creation and the work of a unique creator. Which is as far as individualism and uniqueness can possibly go! And we should naturally expect such a cosmogony to have far-reaching consequences in the psychology and institutions of the people. This is not the place, however, to go into that. But we should at least notice in passing the fierce egalitarianism (less charitable people would have other names for it, of course) which was such a marked feature of Igbo political organization and may justifiably speculate on its possible derivation from this concept of every man's original and absolute uniqueness. An American anthropologist who studied the Igbo community of Onitsha in recent years called his book *The King in Every Man.*[3]

All this might lead one to think that among the Igbo the individual would be supreme, totally free, and existentially alone. But the Igbo are unlikely to concede to the individual an absolutism they deny even to chi. The obvious curtailment of a man's power to walk alone and do as he will is provided by another potent force—the will of his community. For wherever Something stands, no matter what, Something Else will stand beside it. No man, however great, can win judgment against all the people.

We must now turn to the all-important relationship between chi and Chi Ukwu, one of the names by which the Supreme Deity is known in Igbo. Chi Ukwu (or simply,

[3] Richard Henderson, *The King in Every Man.* New Haven: Yale University Press, 1971.

Chukwu) means literally Great Chi. Thus whatever chi may be it does seem to partake of the nature of the Supreme God. Another link is provided by the sun, bringer of daylight. As we saw earlier, among the Igbo of Awka, a man's chi may be invoked to descend from the solar realm. As it happens, the Igbo also see the sun as an agent of Chukwu to whom it is said to bear those rare sacrifices offered as man's last desperate resort. It would seem then that wherever the abode of Chukwu happens to be in the heavens it cannot be distant from the place of chi.

In Yoruba[4] cosmology the Supreme God, Olodumare (one of whose titles is, incidentally, Owner of the Sun), sent the god, Obatala, on a mission of creation to make man. The Igbo are not so specific about Chukwu's role in the creation of man but may be suggesting a similar delegation of power by the Supreme Overlord to a lesser divinity except that in their case every act of creation is the work of a separate and individual agent, chi, a personified and unique manifestation of the creative essence.

Still farther west, the Akan of Ghana believe in a moon goddess whom they call Ngame, Mother of the World, who gives a "soul" to every human being at birth by shooting lunar rays into him. The Igbo, seemingly more reticent about such profound events, may yet be hinting at a comparable cosmic relationship between their chi and solar rays. This would explain the invocation of chi from the face of the sun at the consecration of its shrine and account also for the second meaning of the word: daylight. And, of course, the Igbo being patrilineal (as anthropologists tell us) where the Akan are matrilineal, a

[4] The Yoruba of Western Nigeria are, in size and achievement, among the great peoples of Africa.

preference by them for the sun over the moon would be completely in character!

The significance of the sun in Igbo religion though subtle and unobtrusive is nonetheless undeniable and may even be called pervasive. If we are to believe the New Larousse Encyclopaedia of Mythology, it seems that two-times-two-times-two is everywhere the sun's mystical figure (just as three-times-three is the moon's). Certainly the Igbo have a lot of use for fours and eights. The basic unit of their calendar is the four-day "small" week and an eight-day "great" week; the circumcision of their male child takes place on the eighth day after which it is accounted a human being; they compute largeness in units of four hundred, *nnu,* etc., etc.

The exact relationship between the Supreme God (Chukwu), the sun, and chi in Igbo cosmology will probably never be (and perhaps was intended not to be) unraveled. But if Chukwu means literally Great Chi, one is almost tempted to borrow the words of Christian dogma and speak of chi as being of the same "substance" as, and "proceeding" from, Chukwu. Or is chi an infinitesimal manifestation of Chukwu's infinite essence given to each of us separately and uniquely, a single ray from the sun's boundless radiance? Or does Chukwu have a separate existence as ruler over a community of chi, countless as the stars and as endless in their disparate identities, holding anarchy at bay with His will?

One last word about Chineke which we have come to interpret as *God who creates* and use as an alternative name for Chukwu. If our interpretation and use were supported by Igbo language and religious tradition, the role of Chukwu as *the* Creator would be established and the activity of chi in their multiplicity relegated to the status of mere figure of speech. Unfortunately the early missionaries who appropriated Chineke as the Creator-God of Christianity acted a little hastily, unaware that the Igbo language was capable of treachery to hasty users on account of its tonality. (The story of the white preacher who kept saying that God had great buttocks when he meant great strength may be apocryphal, but it makes an important point.)

Chineke consists of three words: chi na eke. In assigning a meaning to it the crucial word is *na*, which itself has three possible meanings. Let us examine each meaning in turn and see what it does to Chineke:

a) said with a high tone, na means *who* or *which*. Chineke will then mean *chi which creates;*

b) said with a low tone, na can mean the auxiliary verb *does*, in which case Chineke will mean *chi does create;* and finally

c) again said with a low tone, na can mean the conjunctive *and*. Here something fundamental changes because eke is no longer a verb but a noun. Chineke then becomes chi and eke. And that, in my opinion, is the correct version.

Chineke which we have come to interpret as *chi who creates* is nothing of the sort, but rather is a dual deity, chi and eke. The early missionaries by putting the wrong tone on that little word na escorted a two-headed, pagan god into their holy of holies!

Now what are the grounds for making such a terrible assertion? Quite simply I have looked at traditional Igbo usage. But before I give the examples that will make this clear let us take a quick look at eke, this mysterious second member of the duality. What is it? I do not know for certain, but it does seem to have more or less the same attributes as chi; also it is sometimes called *aka*.

We have already referred to the common name Chinwuba (chi has increase) earlier on. Another version of this name is Ekejiuba (eke holds increase). We have also mentioned the name Nebechi (look to chi). Now, there is also Lemeke (Leweke) which would appear to be exactly the same name except that eke occurs instead of chi. It is interesting to note that the chi versions of these names occur more in the northern and western parts of Igbo land while the eke names tend to occur more in the southern and eastern parts.

Let us turn for a moment from proper names to other sayings in which chi and eke are yoked together. If you want to curse a man in the most thorough fashion, you curse his chi and his eke (or aka). That really takes care of him!

There is also the well-known little anecdote about the hen. Someone once asked her why it was that from daybreak to sunset she was always scratching the ground for food; was she never satisfied? To which she replied: "You see, my dear fellow, when I wake up in the morning I begin to look for food for my chi. When I am through with that I must then find some for my eke. By the time I finish with that too it is already sunset and I haven't catered for myself!"

From the foregoing it would appear that chi and eke are very closely related deities, perhaps the same god in a twofold manifestation, such as male and female; or the duality may have come into being for the purpose of bringing two dialectal tributaries of Igbo into liturgical union. This last is particularly attractive because there exists a small number of similar "double-headed" phrases, each comprising two words and the conjunctive, both words being of identical meaning but drawn from two basic dialectal areas. Used in this conjunction the words immediately introduce the element of totality into their ordinary meaning. Thus *ikwu na ibe* stands for the entire community of kinsmen and women; *ogbo na uke* for the militant and aggressive band of spirit adversaries; *okwu na uka* for endless wranglings; *nta na imo* for odds and ends, etc. If indeed *chi na eke* should turn out to belong to this group of phrases, the idea of using it to curse a man absolutely would then make a lot of sense! Which might be bad news indeed for the Christian church in Igbo land. But it may surely draw consolation from the fact that the Book of the Old Testament itself, in all its glory and dignity, ends "with a curse"!

Far be it from me, however, to suggest that Chineke should be dropped at this late hour as an alternative name for Chukwu. That would be futile pedantry; for whatever doubts we may entertain about its antecedents, it has certainly served generations of Christians and non-Christians in Igbo land in contemplating the nature of the all-distant Supreme Deity, whose role in the world is shrouded in mystery and metaphor. The attraction of Chineke for the early evangelists must have been its seeming lack of ambiguity on the all-important question of creation. They needed a "God who creates" and Chineke stood ready at hand. But Igbo traditional thought in its own way and style did recognize Chukwu as the Supreme Creator, speculating only on the modalities, on *how* He accomplished the work and through what agencies and intermediaries. As we have seen He appears to work through chi to create man. Similarly there are numerous suggestions in Igbo lore of Him working with man to make

the world—or rather to enhance its habitability, for the
work of creation was not ended in one monumental effort
but goes on still, Chukwu and man talking things over at
critical moments, sometimes agreeing, sometimes not.
Two examples will suffice:

When Death first came into the world, men sent a messenger to Chukwu to beg Him to remove the terrible
scourge. Although He was disposed to consider the matter, the first request that actually got through to Him from
mankind was the wrong one and once He had granted it
there was no way it could be altered.

In a study of Igbo people published in 1913, Northcote
Thomas recorded the following story about Ezenri, that
fascinating priest/king whose spiritual pre-eminence was
acknowledged over considerable parts of Igbo land:

> Ezenri and Ezadama came from heaven and rested
> on an ant heap; all was water. Cuku (Chukwu) asked
> who was sitting there and they answered "We are the
> kings of Nri and Adama," thereupon Cuku gave them
> each a piece of yam; yams were at that time unknown
> to man, for human beings walked in the bush like
> animals. . . .[5]

Later on Chukwu tells Ezenri how to plant and tend the
yam, but Ezenri complains that the ground is too wet;
and Chukwu advises him to send for Awka people—workers in iron—to blow on the earth with their bellows and
make it dry.

There is a very strong suggestion here, and also in

[5] Northcote W. Thomas, *Ibo-speaking Peoples of Nigeria.* London:
Harrison & Sons, 1913, vol. I; reprinted Negro Universities Press, New
York, 1969, p. 50.

the story about the coming of death, that at crucial cosmological moments Chukwu will discuss His universe with man. The moment of man's first awareness of the implications of death was such a time; but so also was the great turning point when man ceased wandering in the bush and became a settled agriculturist calling upon the craft of the blacksmith to effect this momentous transition.

And finally, at the root of it all lies that very belief we have already seen: a belief in the fundamental worth and independence of every man and of his right to speak on matters of concern to him and, flowing from it, a rejection of any form of absolutism which might endanger those values. It is not surprising that the Igbo held discussion and consensus as the highest ideals of the political process. This made them "argumentative" and difficult to rule. But how could they suspend, for the convenience of a ruler, limitations which they impose even on their gods? For as we have seen, a man may talk and bargain even with his chi at the moment of his creation. And what was more, Chukwu Himself in all His power and glory did not make the world by fiat. He held conversations with mankind; he talked with those archetypal men of Nri and Adama and even enlisted their good offices to make the earth firm and productive.